Kings of Rome:
Early Roman History
in Byzantine Greek

Jōannēs Zōnarās *scrīpsit*

Erik Robinson *in linguam Anglicam vertit ēdiditque*

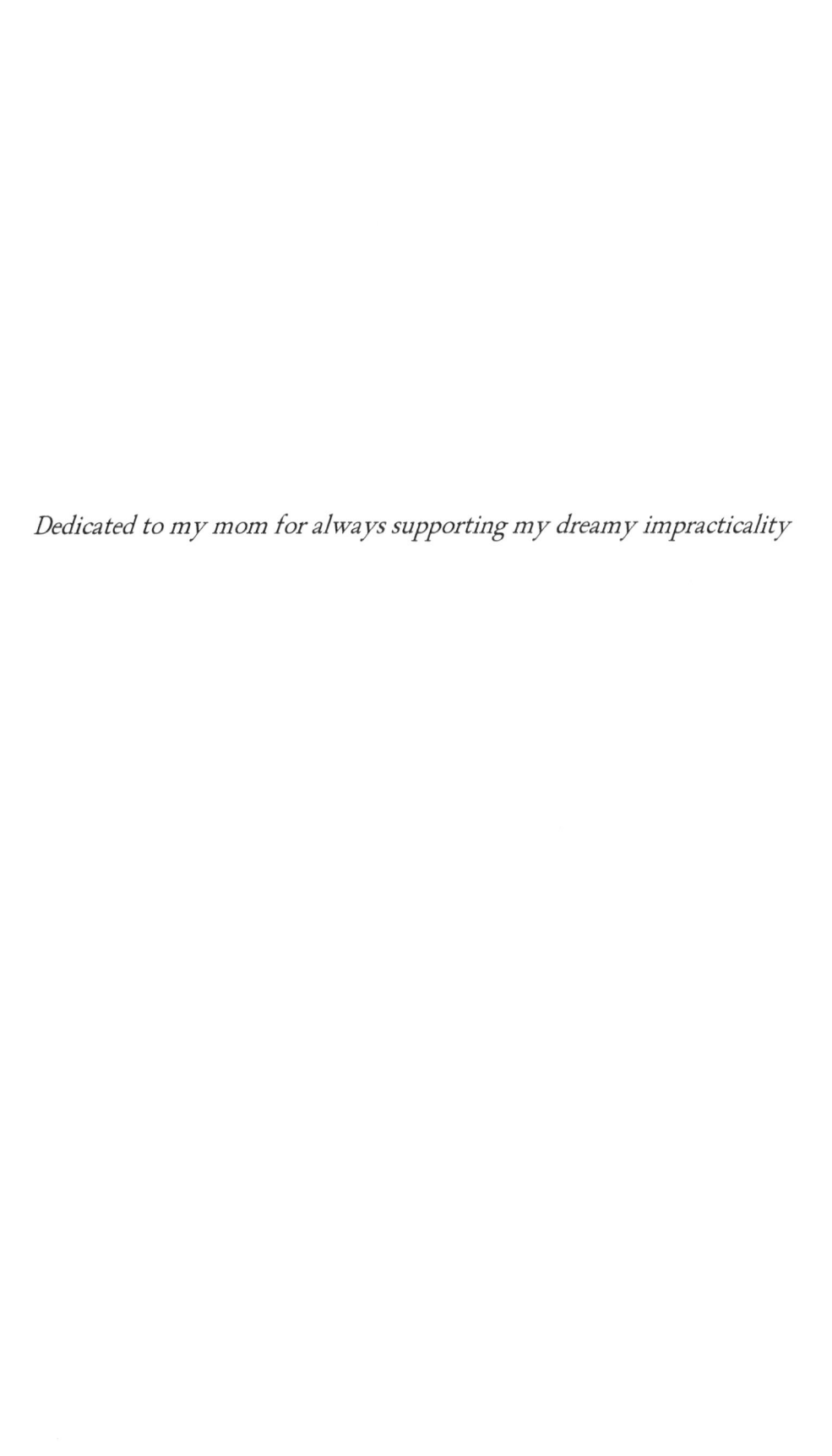

Dedicated to my mom for always supporting my dreamy impracticality

Ioannes Zonaras, c. 1070 – c. 1140

16ᵗʰ-Century Engraving

Index Capitulōrum

Praefātiō

Ioannes Zonaras is not, even among the learned, a name often raised in conversation or read on the page. The book which you hold in your hands constitutes a small selection from Zonaras' *Epitome of Histories*, a work which attempts to summarize the history of the world beginning with the creation story of *Genesis* and culminates in the events of Zonaras' own life in the 12th century CE. It is a massive work for a massive subject: from God's fashioning of the world to the death of Alexios Komnenos. His aim is best captured by the line in Ovid's proem to the *Metamorphoses: prīmāque ab orīgine mundī / ad mea perpetuum dēdūcite tempora carmen!* ("Lead the thread of my song from the origin of the world down to my times." Metamorphoses 1.3-4) Yet, despite the grand ambition of this chronicle, Zonaras himself suggests in his introduction that it is a *parergon*, or side project, rather than his main business: "Someone could justly mock me by saying that my side project (parergon) is greater than my work (ergon)."[1]

Life of Zonaras

Though we have a not insignificant amount of material from Zonaras' pen, comparatively little about his life can be stated with certainty. This is a particular problem in Byzantine history,

---

[1] Εὐστόχως ἄν τις εἴποι ἐπιτωθάζων μοι, μεῖζόν σοι τοῦ ἔργου τὸ πάρεργον. [Zonaras, *Epitome* - Proem]

which presents scholars with substantial *lacunae* in record keeping and documentary evidence.

It seems that Zonaras was born around 1080 CE, and based on references within his Canon commentaries, he died sometime after 1161.[2] He was likely given the standard education for civil servants, consisting of rhetorical and literary training combined with legalistic studies. In his career as a civil servant, he held the position of *protasēcrêtis* (πρωτασηκρῆτις) or chief imperial notary. (This title itself reflects the Roman inheritance of Byzantine culture, since it is a Hellenized form of the Latin title for imperial notaries, a *sēcrētis.*) He also served as a *droungários* (δρουγγάριος) of the watch, a high-level military post. After the death of Alexios I Komnenos, Zonaras may have backed Anna Komnene against John II Komnenos, necessitating his entry into monastic life when the latter ascended to the throne.[3] This was about two decades before the publication of the *Epitome* in 1143. As was the case with figures like Thucydides and Cicero in antiquity, a forced withdrawal from public life proved to be an impetus for a fruitful authorial career. Ultimately, as is the case with many pre-modern writers, most of what we know about Zonaras is the work itself. Here we will bear in mind that classic of Wittgensteinian advice and remain silent on matters of which we cannot speak.

Byzantine Historiography - Epitome and Chronicle

Zonaras' *Epitome* owes its structure and aims to two historiographic trends. The first is the epitome as a genre stemming

---

[2] Kampianaki, Theofili: *Epitome of Histories: A Compendium of Jewish-Roman History and Its Reception.* Oxford: Oxford University Press (2022): 13
[3] Ibid.: 14

from antiquity and best represented by Florus' *Epitome of Roman History*, a slick and concise abridgement of Livy's voluminous *ab Urbe Conditā*. These condensed versions of longer historical works are not prized for their originality or insight; rather, they are handy surveys for the busy reader who wanted simply to have a broad stroke outline of a given historical work or period.

The second, more properly Byzantine, mode of historiography is the *chronicle.* Cyril Mango describes the genre of chronicles thus:

> *[...] written in everyday language, it was meant to provide an overview of everything that had happened since the Creation of the world down to the compiler's own lifetime. Its entries, arranged chronologically, tended to be brief and did not present events in a causal nexus. The chronicle was considered an edifying rather than a literary work, which meant that it was progressively updated and re-edited, while older versions were often discarded.[4]*

Zonaras' book can be thought of as a chronicle composed largely of epitomes. In the arena of Roman history, a substantial chunk of Zonaras' account seems to have relied heavily on Cassius Dio. By beginning at the creation, pious and patriotic chroniclers were able to frame history in theo-teleological terms, whereby the entire course of human history had led inexorably down to their own times. Zonaras, a monk who had formerly had a senior administrative position in the government, reflects his two careers in the material of his text, concerned as it is with the imperial and the theological.

---

[4] Cyril Mango, *The Oxford History of Byzantium* (New York: Oxford University Press, 2002)

Although the selection offered here begins with the mythical prehistory of Rome, astute readers will note that this excerpt begins at Book VII of the *Epitome*. The first six books were entirely devoted to Jewish history as laid out in the standard Biblical version. While there is a sort of directional narrative momentum uniting the entirety of the Epitome, it is, in effect, capable of a tripartite division: Jewish antiquities, Roman history, Byzantine history. Of course, the division between the "Roman" and "Byzantine" sections is one that *we* might make today under the influence of the belief that "Rome" ceased to be either with the deposition of Romulus Augustulus, the reign of Justinian, or the reign of Heraclius, all of which have been proposed as points at which Byzantine history begins. Zonaras would have made no such distinction: Constantinople was the seat of the Roman empire to him, so the shift from Jewish antiquities to the treatment of Rome which begins in Book VII of the *Epitome* is meant to form a unitary whole leading from Romulus to Alexios I Komnenos.

While classicizing Byzantine historians may have tried to model themselves on either Herodotus (broad, digressive history with wide-ranging ethnographic interest) or Thucydides (minute and detailed investigation of a narrow time period, replete with analysis), these approaches tended to be applied to works dealing only with Byzantine affairs and not to the rehashing of ancient historical accounts. Perhaps the most striking omission effected by Zonaras' tunnel vision is the omission of sustained Greek history. There is perhaps some irony in a historian writing in Greek who largely neglects the glories of ancient Hellas, but this may be taken as an indication of how central "Roman" identity still was to the identity of the Byzantines in the 12th century.

Most of Zonaras' *Epitome* is not notable as a work of profound genius or originality. While it is true that some of the Byzantine sections of his history are valuable because they preserve information about the 11th and 12th centuries which would otherwise be lost or very lightly documented. Rather, as is the case with most *epitomes* from antiquity, its chief merits are its allusive preservation of source material which is now lost, and its revelation of what learned Byzantines of the 12th century knew, or thought they knew, about the history of civilization.

On the former point: much of the reconstructive work which has been done on the first 21 books of Cassius Dio's *Roman History* has relied on Zonaras, who drew heavily on Dio for the time period (from Rome's founding through the Punic Wars) covered in those lost books. Indeed, we can even glean some information about the state of Dio's work in the 12th century from what Zonaras omits. His relatively light treatment of Late Republican history can be chalked up to his inability to consult Dio on this period.[5] But his value for students of Dio cannot be overstated: there are sections of Dio's work (for example, chapter 65, covering the reign of Vitellius) which we know only through Zonaras.[6]

Although Zonaras is eminently useful in the reconstruction of lost content of Dio, he drew on several other sources (Josephus, for example) for his narrative. The scholarly consensus is that, despite differences in language and depth of treatment, the actual material as presented by Zonaras is faithful to its origins in Dio's

[5] Kampianaki, *Epitome of Histories: A Compendium of Jewish-Roman History and Its Reception:* 28

[6] Caillan Davenport. "The Conduct of Vitellius in Cassius Dio's 'Roman History'." *Historia: Zeitschrift für Alte Geschichte* 63, no. 1 (2014): 102

work.[7] For some periods, this may not be owing to Zonaras' study of Dio's text itself, but instead to his reliance on the *Epitome* of Xiphilinus (11th century), his predecessor in the summary condensation of ancient Roman history. Xiphilinus was more of an epitomator than a chronicler. Indeed, a comparison of Xiphilinus and Zonaras serves to clearly illustrate the difference between the modes of epitome and chronicle. Whereas Zonaras' book treats the entire course of human history, Xiphilinus produced an abridgement of books 36-80 of Cassius Dio, covering the period from Pompey to the reign of Alexander Severus. Xiphilinus' approach is much more limited than Zonaras', not only in its temporal restriction, but also in its exclusive mission to summarize one piece of work rather than to provide a coherent account of all of creation.

Although the Byzantines thought of themselves as lineal successors to Rome, the 11th and 12th centuries were a period of fervent anti-Latin sentiment in Constantinople, culminating in the Massacre of the Latins in 1182, just two decades after Zonaras' death. In light of this anti-Latin sentiment, it is not entirely surprising that certain elements of the distant Roman past get slightly bungled in the *Epitome*, as for example when Romulus' brother is called "Romus." But we ought to resist the temptation to laugh at the state of Zonaras' knowledge on account of these little mistakes. Much of the early history of Rome which Zonaras covers in these selections is, even among writers like Livy who were much closer to the source material, a variable contexture of fictions and historical *lacunae*, and we ought to bear in mind that Zonaras was separated from the period of Roman monarchy by a larger gulf of

---

[7] Davenport. "The Conduct of Vitellius in Cassius Dio's 'Roman History'." 98

time than that which separates us from Zonaras.

Some of Zonaras' errors and surprising claims are precisely what make his history worth reading, if not for the definitive historical account of Roman history, then at least for an insight into the state of Classical scholarship in 12th century Constantinople. As Nicholas S. M. Matheou notes, Zonaras' *Epitome* is "an ideal case study for how Constantinople was understood in East Roman thought of the central medieval era."[8] Indeed, Livy himself expressed some skepticism about the possibility of disentangling historical fact from legend for this poorly documented early period:

> *It is not my intention to affirm or to refute those things which are related to have occurred before the founding of the city and are more properly suited as ornaments to poetic stories than to the uncorrupted monuments of historical writing. But we grant this privilege to antiquity of mixing the human and the divine to make the origins of cities appear more respectable.[9]*

Elsewhere, Livy includes various asides meant to undercut the traditional legend with a healthy dose of naturalist reasoning, as for example when he attempts to explain the story of Romulus and Remus being nursed by a she-wolf by noting that "lupa" meant not just "she-wolf" but also "prostitute." From this he concludes

---

[8] Nicholas Matheou, "City and Sovereignty in East Roman Thought, c. 1000 - 1200: Ioannes Zonaras' Historical Vision of the Roman State." *The Medieval Mediterranean*, 106 (2016): 42

[9] ...quae ante conditam condendamve urbem poēticīs magis decōra fābulīs quam incorruptīs rērum gestārum monumentīs trāduntur, ea nec adfirmāre nec refellere in animō est. Datur haec venia antīquitātī ut miscendō hūmāna dīvīnīs prīmōrdia urbium augustiōra faciat...

that early reception of the tale confused the two senses of the word and glossed over Acca Larentia's occupation in favor of the mythic and legendary wolf tale. (This explanation gets picked up and incorporated in the *Epitome,* too.) Even when we read these stories in Livy, we are aware that we are not reading "history", but we understand that these tales provide us with an important insight into what the Romans believed, or at least circulated, about their history. And so, even if the reader is familiar with the broad outlines of the history of the Roman monarchy from Livy and others, they may find it illuminating to flip through Zonaras to see how these tales were understood in the 12th century before the methods of modern scholarship pieced together what little we know for certain about this period.

Other Works

Zonaras also wrote some ecclesiastical poetry and various small explications of the ecclesiastical poetry of others. There is a *Lexicon* of the 13th century to which the name of Zonaras was appended and which was, in a more credulous age, believed to be his work, but the obvious chronological problem with this attribution permits swift dismissal.

It seems, then, that Zonaras' side project was grander than his primary, ecclesiastical work. Though there may not be much *novelty* in Zonaras, he is still a concise and interesting author writing in a nostalgically clear, classicizing Greek. The beginning of this introduction noted that he is rarely read today, but we hope that this small selection goes some way to change that.

SELECT BIBLIOGRAPHY

Afinogenov, Dmitry E. "Some Observations on Genres of Byzantine Historiography." *Byzantion* 62 (1992): 13-33

Buttrey, T.V. "Dio, Zonaras and the Value of the Roman Aureus." *The Journal of Roman Studies* 51, parts 1 and 2 (1961): 40-45

Davenport, Caillan. "The Conduct of Vitellius in Cassius Dio's 'Roman History'." *Historia: Zeitschrift für Alte Geschichte* 63, no. 1 (2014): 96-116

Dickey, Eleanor. *Ancient Greek Scholarship.* Oxford: Oxford University Press, 2007.

Kampianaki, Theofili: *Epitome of Histories: A Compendium of Jewish-Roman History and Its Reception.* Oxford: Oxford University Press, 2022.

Lilie, Ralph-Johannes. "Reality and Invention: Reflections on Byzantine Historiography." *Dumbarton Oaks Papers*, 68 (2014): 157-210

Mango, Cyril. *The Oxford History of Byzantium.* New York: Oxford University Press, 2002.

Matheou, Nicholas S.M. "City and Sovereignty in East Roman Thought, c. 1000 - 1200: Ioannes Zonaras' Historical Vision of the Roman State." *The Medieval Mediterranean*, 106 (2016): 41-63

Neville, Leonora. *Guide to Byzantine Historical Writing.* Cambridge: Cambridge University Press, 2018

Ostrogorsky, George, *History of the Byzantine State.* New Brunswick: Rutgers University Press, 1969.

Sandys, John Edwin. *A History of Classical Scholarship: Volume I.* Cambridge: Cambridge University Press, 1903.

7.1

Aeneas

Since mention has been made of the history of the Romans, including their unconquerable strength, it is absolutely necessary to say and teach, or at least to recall those who are recorded in that book, and who these Romans were, and whence their race originally sprang, how they got their name, what sort of government they employed, what fortunes they enjoyed, and how they progressed to the highest point of happiness when they commanded but a tiny portion of the inhabited world and restrained the power of nearly all others; further, how they proceeded from their original monarchy to an aristocracy (that is, the dictatorship and the consulship), then to democracy, and finally back to monarchy. I must therefore discourse upon these things and set out in detail as much as it is possible for one trying to cut the wide breadth, and manage the tediousness, of such a wide subject, so that all pertaining to the history may be readily intelligible and not escape the memory of posterity.

Following the Trojan War, Aeneas came to the Aborigines, who first inhabited the region where Rome was founded, and where Latinus, the son of Faunus, then ruled. He continued on to Laurentum, near the river Numicium, where it is said that he prepared to found his city in accordance with a certain oracle. But Latinus, who was then the king of that land, prevented Aeneas from establishing a foundation there, and when it came to blows he was beaten. They were then reconciled by dreams which appeared to each of them. Latinus conceded the right of settlement to Aeneas, and even gave him his daughter Lavinia in marriage, for which reason Aeneas named the city which he founded Lavinium. The region was called Latium and

7.1

Αἰνείας

Ῥωμαίων δὲ μνησθείσης τῆς ἱστορίας καὶ τούτοις κράτος ἀναθεμένης ἀήττητον, ἀναγκαῖον πάντως εἰπεῖν καὶ διδάξαι ἢ ἀναμνῆσαι τοὺς ἐντευξομένους τούτῳ δὴ τῷ συγγράμματι τίνες τε οἱ Ῥωμαῖοι καὶ ὅθεν τὸ τούτων ἔθνος συνέστη τὸ ἐξ ἀρχῆς, καὶ πόθεν τὴν κλῆσιν ἔσχε, καὶ τίσι πολιτείαις ἐχρήσατο, καὶ οἵαις τύχαις ἐνέκυρσε, καὶ ὅπως προύκοψεν εἰς εὐδαιμονίας ἀκρότητα ὡς μικροῦ κυριεῦσαι τῆς οἰκουμένης ἁπάσης καὶ τὸ κράτος κατὰ πάντων σχεδὸν ἀναδήσασθαι, καὶ ὅπως βασιλευθὲν ἐξ ἀρχῆς εἰς ἀριστοκρατίαν ἤτοι δικτατωρείας καὶ ὑπατείας μετέπεσε, καὶ εἰς δημοκρατίαν αὖθις μετήνεκτο, εἶτα εἰς μοναρχίαν ἐπανελήλυθεν. ῥητέον μοι τοίνυν καὶ περὶ τούτων καὶ διηγητέον ὡς ἐνὸν ἐπιτέμνοντι τὸ πλάτος τῆς διηγήσεως καὶ τὴν μακρη γορίαν συστέλλοντι, ἵν’ εἶεν εὐσύνοπτα τὰ τῆς ἱστορίας καὶ τὴν τῶν ἐπιόντων μνήμην μὴ διαφεύγοιεν.

Αἰνείας μετὰ τὸν Τρωικὸν πόλεμον ἀφῖκτο πρὸς ’Αβορίγινας, οἳ πρῴην τὴν χώραν ᾤκουν καθ’ ἣν ἡ Ῥώμη πεπόλισται, Λατίνου τοῦ Φαύνου τότε τὴν τούτων ἀρχὴν ἔχοντος, καὶ προσέσχε Λαυρεντῷ κατὰ τὸν Νουμίκιον ποταμόν, ἔνθα κατά τι δὴ θεοπρόπιον λέγεται παρασκευάζεσθαι ποιήσασθαι τὴν κατοίκησιν. ὁ δὲ τῆς χώρας ἄρχων Λατῖνος ἀπεῖργε τῷ Αἰνείᾳ τὴν ἐν τῇ χώρᾳ καθίδρυσιν. καὶ συμβαλὼν ἡττᾶται· εἶτα δι’ ὀνειράτων φανέντων ἀμφοῖν καταλάττονται· καὶ τῆς κατοικίας αὐτῷ παραχωρεῖ, καὶ τὴν θυγα τέρα Λαουινίαν εἰς γάμον ἐκδίδωσιν. ἔνθα πόλιν ὁ Αἰνείας οἰκοδομήσας ὠνόμασε Λαουίνιον· ἥ τε χώρα Λάτιον ἐπεκλήθη καὶ οἱ ἄνθρωποι οἱ ἐκεῖ

the people who lived there were then called Latins.

But the neighboring Rutulians set out from their city of Ardea and since they were previously ill-disposed toward the Latins, they then initiated a war with the help of Turnus, a man both noble and formerly allied with Latinus. He had, however, become enraged with Latinus on account of Lavinia's marriage, because she was previously promised to him. During the war, both Turnus and Latinus fell, and Aeneas won both the victory and his father-in-law's throne. After a little time, however, the Rutulians received some aid from the Tyrsenians and came up against Aeneas again, this time winning the war. Aeneas disappeared, and since he was never again seen either living or dead, he was honored among the Latins as a god. Therefore, the Romans consider him their founder, and they boastfully call themselves the children of Aeneas *(Aeneidae)*. Aeneas' son Ascanius, who had followed his father from Troy, then assumed the throne, for Aeneas had not yet had a child with Lavinia, though he did leave her pregnant at his death. The enemy then surrounded Ascanius and besieged him, but the Latins set upon them at night and ended both the siege and the war.

After some time had passed and the Latins had increased the population of Lavinium, most of them left the city and founded another one in a more agreeable region, which they called Alba Longa – Alba because of its whiteness, and Longa because of its magnitude. Upon the death of Ascanius, the Latins honored the son born to Aeneas from Lavinia (named Silvius) over and above the son of Ascanius, preferring Silvius because Latinus was his grandfather. An Aeneas was born to Silvius, from this Aeneas was born another Latinus, and Pastis succeeded this Latinus. A man named Tiberinus, setting out on the river named Albulus, fell in and died. This river was afterward called the

Λατῖνοι προσηγορεύθησαν.

Ῥουτοῦλοι δὲ ὁμοροῦντες τῇ χώρᾳ ἐκ πόλεως Ἀρδέας ὁρμώμενοι, καὶ πρόσθεν δυσμενῶς ἔχοντες πρὸς Λατίνους, καὶ τότε πόλεμον ἤραντο, ἐπαρήγοντος αὐτοῖς καὶ Τούρνου ἀνδρὸς ἐπιφανοῦς καὶ τῷ Λατίνῳ προσήκοντος, ὃς δι᾽ ὀργῆς τὸν Λατῖνον πεποίητο διὰ τὸν Λαουινίας γάμον· ἐκείνῳ γὰρ ἡ κόρη προωμολόγητο. μάχης οὖν γενομένης πίπτουσιν ὅ τε Τοῦρνος καὶ ὁ Λατῖνος, τὴν δὲ νίκην ὁ Αἰνείας ἐκόμιστο καὶ τὴν τοῦ πενθεροῦ βασιλείαν. μετὰ δέ τινα χρόνον συμμαχίας ἐκ Τυρσηνῶν οἱ Ῥουτοῦλοι τυχόντες ἐπῆλθον τῷ Αἰνείᾳ, καὶ τὸν πόλεμον νενικήκασιν· ἀφανὴς δὲ ὁ Αἰνείας γενόμενος, οὔτε γὰρ ζῶν ὤφθη ἔτι οὔτε μὴν τεθνεώς, ὡς θεὸς παρὰ Λατίνοις τετίμητο. ἐντεῦθεν καὶ τοῖς Ῥωμαίοις τοῦ σφετέρου γένους ἀρχηγέτης νενόμισται, καὶ Αἰνειάδαι καλεῖσθαι αὐχοῦσι. τὴν δὲ τῶν Λατίνων ἀρχὴν ὁ ἐκείνου υἱὸς Ἀσκάνιος διεδέξατο, ὃς οἴκοθεν συνείπετο τῷ πατρί· οὐδέπω γὰρ ἐκ τῆς Λαουινίας παῖδα ἐγείνατο, ἔγκυον δ᾽ αὐτὴν καταλέλοιπε. τὸν δὲ Ἀσκάνιον κατακλείσαντες οἱ πολέμιοι ἐπολιόρκουν· νυκτὸς δ᾽ οἱ Λατῖνοι αὐτοῖς ἐπιθέμενοι τήν τε πολιορκίαν ἔλυσαν καὶ τὸν πόλεμον.

Χρόνου δὲ διεληλυθότος πληθυνθέντες οἱ Λατῖνοι τὴν μὲν πόλιν τὸ Λαουίνιον οἱ πλείονες ἐκλελοίπασιν, ἑτέραν δ᾽ ἐν ἀμείνονι χώρᾳ ἀντῳκοδόμησαν, ἣν Ἄλβαν ἐκ τῆς λευκότητος καὶ ἀπὸ τοῦ μήκους Λόγγαν ἐπωνόμασαν· εἴποιεν ἂν Ἕλληνες λευκὴν καὶ μακράν. Ἀσκανίου δὲ τελευτήσαντος οἱ Λατῖνοι τὸν ἐκ τῆς Λαουινίας τεχθέντα τῷ Αἰνείᾳ υἱὸν εἰς τὴν βασιλείαν προετιμήσαντο τοῦ Ἀσκανίου παιδός, διὰ τὸν πάππον τὸν Λατῖνον τοῦτον προκρίναντες, Σιλούιον κεκλημένον. ἐκ Σιλουίου δὲ Αἰνείας ἐτέχθη, ἐξ Αἰνείου δὲ Λατῖνος ἐγένετο, Λατῖνον δὲ διεδέξατο Πάστις. Τιβερῖνος δ᾽ ἄρξας μετέπειτα ἐν ποταμῷ καλουμένῳ Ἀλβούλῳ πεσὼν διεφθάρη· ὃς δὴ ποταμὸς

Tiber after him; it flowed through Rome, provided a most excellent supply to the city, and was useful to the Romans in the highest degree. Amulius, the son of Tiberinus, who became exceedingly arrogant and attempted to deify himself, died while trying to return lightning against lightning by means of a contrivance, and even to make the light flash and hurl thunderbolts. The pond near which his palace was built suddenly began to flow and swept both Amulius and his palace into the sea. Then, Amulius' son Aventinus was killed in battle.

So much for Lavinium and the Albans. Roman affairs had as their beginning Numitor and Amulius, who were the sons of Aventinus, and the descendants of Aeneas. Once the throne in Alba Longa had fallen to them through succession, they wished to apportion it out between themselves, along with the royal possessions. When Amulius set both the property and the crown as private, and asked his brother which of the two he would like for himself, Numitor chose the crown because he was the older brother. Amulius took the property and surrounded himself with the power which naturally attends wealth, and with it seized the crown. Numitor had a daughter and Amulius, fearing that she might have children who would rebel against him, made her a priestess of Hestia which entailed that she would be an unmarried virgin through all of her life. She was seen later to be pregnant by Ares, as the myth goes, but most probably it was by some man. She was imprisoned on that account, so that she could not escape when she gave birth. She gave birth to two children who were great and noble. Amulius, now even more terrified, ordered that the children be cast out. So, he took them and placed them in a little cradle in the Tiber. The water's flow led the cradle away to a pleasant spot, where they say that a she-wolf came upon the children and offered

Τίβερις ἐξ ἐκείνου μετωνομάσθη, ῥέων διὰ τῆς Ῥώμης καὶ ὢν τῇ πόλει πολυαρκέστατος καὶ Ῥωμαίοις ἐς τὰ μάλιστα χρησιμώτατος. ἔκγονος δὲ τοῦ Τιβερίνου Ἀμούλιος, ὃς ὑπερφρονήσας καὶ θεοῦν ἑαυτὸν τολμήσας, ὡς βροντάς τε ταῖς βρονταῖς ἐκ μηχανῆς ἀντεπάγειν καὶ ἀνταστράπτειν ταῖς ἀστραπαῖς ἐνσκήπτειν τε κεραυνούς, διεφθάρη, τῆς λίμνης παρ᾽ ᾗ τὰ αὐτοῦ βασίλεια ἵδρυτο ἐπιρρυείσης αἰφνίδιον καὶ καταποντισάσης κἀκεῖνον καὶ τὰ βασίλεια. Ἀουεντῖνος δὲ ὁ υἱὸς αὐτοῦ ἐν πολέμῳ ἀπέθανε.

Καὶ ταῦτα μὲν περὶ Λαουινίου καὶ Ἀλβανῶν· τὰ δὲ τῶν Ῥωμαίων ἀρχὴν ἐσχήκασι τὸν Νομίτωρά τε καὶ τὸν Ἀμούλιον, οἳ Ἀουεντίνου μὲν ἐγένοντο υἱωνοί, τοῦ δ᾽ Αἰνείου ἀπόγονοι. τῆς γοῦν ἐν Ἄλβῃ βασιλείας κατὰ διαδοχὴν περιελθούσης αὐτοῖς, νείμασθαι ταύτην ἠθέλησαν καὶ τὰ χρήματα. τοῦ Ἀμουλίου τοίνυν ἰδίᾳ μὲν τὰ χρήματα θέντος, ἰδίᾳ δέ γε τὴν βασιλείαν, καὶ ἐξ ἀμφοῖν τὸν ἀδελφὸν προτρεψαμένου ὃ πρὸς βουλῆς αὐτῷ ἐπιλέξασθαι, τὴν βασιλείαν εἵλετο ὁ Νομίτωρ, ἅτε καὶ πρεσβύτερος ἀδελφός· λαβὼν δὲ τὰ χρήματα ὁ Ἀμούλιος, καὶ δύναμιν ἐκ τούτων περιβαλλόμενος, καὶ τὴν βασιλείαν ἀφείλετο. θυγατρὸς δὲ τῷ Νομίτωρι οὔσης, δεδιὼς μὴ παῖδες ἐξ αὐτῆς γένοιντο καὶ κατεξανασταῖεν αὐτοῦ, ἱέρειαν τῆς Ἑστίας ἐκείνην ἀπέδειξεν, ἄγαμον διὰ τοῦτο καὶ παρθένον διὰ βίου μέλλουσαν ἔσεσθαι. ἡ δὲ κύουσα ἐφωράθη μετέπειτα ὑπὸ Ἄρεος, ὡς μυθεύεται, ὑπ᾽ ἀνθρώπων δὲ πάντως τινός. εἴρχθη οὖν διὰ τοῦτο, ἵνα μὴ λάθῃ τεκοῦσα. καὶ ἔτεκε διδύμους παῖδας μεγάλους τε καὶ καλούς. μᾶλλον οὖν φοβηθεὶς ὁ Ἀμούλιος ἐκέλευσε τὰ βρέφη ῥιφῆναι. καὶ ὁ ταῦτα λαβὼν σκάφῃ ἐνθέμενος ἐμβάλλει τῷ ποταμῷ τῷ Τιβέριδι. παρασῦραν δὲ τὴν σκάφην τὸ ῥεῦμα εἴς τινα χῶρον κατήνεγκε μαλθακόν· ἔνθα κειμένοις τοῖς βρέφεσι λύκαιναν ἱστοροῦσι προσιοῦσαν θηλὴν παρέχειν αὐτοῖς,

them her teat; they also say that there was a woodpecker there feeding them and guarding them. One of Amulius' swineherds, named Faustulus, came upon the children there and took them. He then raised them with his wife, whose name was Larentia. One was named Romulus, and the other Remus. Some deny that a she-wolf nursed them, which would be more credible or even have more of an air of truth, but this story took hold from the beginning. The Romans call both she-wolves and prostitutes *lupas*. The fact that Larentia, who raised the boys, was a prostitute and on that account called a *lupa* (she-wolf) caused the region to submit to the myth.

καὶ ὄρνιν δρυοκολάπτην παρεῖναι ταῦτα ψωμίζοντα καὶ φυλάττοντα. ἐκεῖ δὲ κείμενα τὰ βρέφη λαθὼν ἀφείλετό τις Ἀμουλίου συοφορβὸς Φαυστοῦλος καλούμενος· καὶ παρὰ τῆς ἐκείνου ἐτράφησαν γυναικός, ᾗ ὄνομα Λαρεντία· καὶ ὁ μὲν Ῥωμύλος, ὁ δ' ἕτερος Ῥῶμος ἐκλήθησαν. τινὲς δὲ μὴ λύκαιναν εἶναι τὴν τῶν παίδων φασὶ τροφόν, ὃ καὶ πιθανώτερον ἢ ἀληθέστερον μάλιστα, ἀρχὴν δὲ τὸν λόγον οὕτω λαβεῖν. λούπας καλοῦσι Ῥωμαῖοι τάς τε λυκαίνας καὶ τὰς ἑταίρας· πορνευομένη δ' ἡ Λαρεντία, ἣ τοὺς παῖδας ἐθρέψατο, καὶ λοῦπα διὰ τοῦτο καλουμένη, χώραν τῷ μύθῳ παρέσχετο.

Romulus and Remus

When they grew up, they were both manly and high-spirited. Romulus seemed more distinguished for his intelligence and was more inclined to command than obey. When a dispute arose between the cowherds of Numitor and those of Amulius, the brothers beat them and took a great share of the cattle. The cowherds of Numitor then laid a trap for Remus when he was walking alone with a few others; they captured him and brought him to Numitor. He feared retribution for coming up against Amulius, being his brother and often maltreated by the members of his household. But Amulius gave Remus to Numitor to do with him as he wished. As Numitor was returning home and gazing upon Remus, who was distinguished for his size and strength, he marveled at his boldness and indomitable nature, and then asked him in a low voice who he was and who his parents were. Remus boldly replied, 'We are twin brothers; our lineage is said to be unspeakable, and our rearing and nursing is even more incredible, since we were nursed by beasts and birds after being set in a tiny cradle next to the great river; indeed, it still exists, with some faint words engraved on the bronze ribs which hold it together.'

Numitor was then led on by both the speech and appearance of Remus to think about the exposure of his daughter's children. When Faustulus learned of the capture of Remus, he urged Romulus to help him, and at that time told him clearly about his own lineage which was previously kept secret in order to prevent them from becoming small-minded. He then got the cradle and brought it to Numitor in the full bloom of zeal and anxiety. When he was seen by the guards posted outside the gates of

7.2
Ῥωμύλος καὶ Ῥῶμος

Αὐξανόμενοι δὲ θυμοειδεῖς ἦσαν καὶ ἀνδρώδεις ἀμφότεροι· ὁ δὲ Ῥωμύλος ἐδόκει συνέσει διαφορώτερος καὶ ἡγεμονικὸς μᾶλλον τὴν φύσιν ἢ πειθαρχικός. γενομένης δέ ποτε πρὸς τοὺς Νομίτωρος βουκόλους τοῖς τοῦ Ἀμουλίου διαφορᾶς, συγκόπτουσιν αὐτοὺς οἱ ὁμαίμονες καὶ τῆς ἀγέλης συχνὴν ἀποτέμνονται μοῖραν. μόνῳ δὲ τῷ Ῥώμῳ σὺν ὀλίγοις ἄλλοις βαδίζοντι οἱ τοῦ Νομίτωρος βουκόλοι λοχήσαντες συνέλαβον αὐτὸν καὶ ἀπήγαγον πρὸς Νομίτωρα· καὶ ὃς πρὸς Ἀμούλιον ἐλθὼν ἐδεῖτο τυχεῖν δίκης, ἀδελφὸς ὢν καὶ ὑπὸ τῶν οἰκείων αὐτοῦ ὑβρισμένος. ὁ δὲ παραδίδωσι τῷ Νομίτωρι τὸν Ῥῶμον ὡς βούλοιτο χρήσασθαι. ὃς οἴκοι ἐλθὼν καὶ τὸν νεανίσκον ὁρῶν ὑπερφέροντα μεγέθει καὶ ῥώμῃ, καὶ τὸ θαρραλέον αὐτοῦ καὶ ἀδούλωτον τῆς ψυχῆς θαυμάζων, ἀνέκρινεν ὅστις εἴη καὶ ὅθεν γένοιτο, φωνῇ πραείᾳ. ὁ δὲ θαρρῶν ἔλεγεν ὡς "δίδυμοι μέν ἐσμεν ἀδελφοί, γοναὶ δὲ ἡμῶν ἀπόρρητοι λέγονται καὶ τροφαὶ καὶ τιθηνήσεις θαυμασιώτεραι, θηρίοις καὶ οἰωνοῖς τραφέντων παρὰ τὸν μέγαν ποταμὸν ἐν σκάφῃ τινὶ κειμένων, ἣ ἔτι σώζεται, χαλκοῖς ὑποζώμασι γραμμάτων ἀμυδρῶν ἐγκεχαραγμένων."

Ὁ μὲν οὖν Νομίτωρ τοῖς τε λόγοις τοῦ Ῥώμου καὶ τῇ ὄψει πρὸς ἔννοιαν τῆς ἐκθέσεως τῶν τῆς θυγατρὸς ἐνήγετο παίδων, ὁ δὲ Φαυστοῦλος τὴν τοῦ Ῥώμου μαθὼν σύλληψιν τὸν μὲν Ῥωμύλον βοηθεῖν παρεκάλει, τότε σαφῶς διδάξας αὐτὸν περὶ τῆς γενέσεως, πρότερον γὰρ ὑπηνίττετο, ὥστ' αὐτοὺς μὴ μικροφρονεῖν, αὐτὸς δὲ τὴν σκάφην κομίζων ἐχώρει πρὸς τὸν Νομίτωρα σπουδῆς καὶ δέους μεστός. τοῖς δὲ περὶ τὰς πύλας τοῦ

11

Amulius, and appeared to be anxious under their questioning, it did not escape notice that he was hiding the cradle underneath his mantle. Thinking that he was concealing something which he had stolen, they brought the cradle out into the open. There happened to be present one of the men who had exposed the boys. He recognized the cradle and ran to tell Amulius. When Faustulus was interrogated by the king, he explained that the boys were alive, and further were cowherds in Alba Longa. He brought the cradle to Ilia, the mother of the boys, who wanted to see it. Disturbed by all of this, Amulius sent a man to Numitor to find out whether he could learn anything of the boys, since they were still alive. The man who had been sent on this expedition was one of Numitor's friends. He went away and found Numitor lost in the complicated puzzle about Remus; he then urged Numitor on and counseled that there should be no delay, and he himself helped with the deed. Just then, Romulus arrived with a large band of rustics. A few of the city dwellers had also joined him from hatred of Amulius. Since matters had fallen out thus, Amulius – neither doing nor contriving anything – ran away to save his life.

Ἀμουλίου φρουροῖς ὑφορώμενος, καὶ ταραττόμενος περὶ τὰς ἀποκρίσεις, οὐκ ἔλαθε τὴν σκάφην τῷ χλανιδίῳ περικαλύπτων. ὑπολαβόντες δὲ κλοπιμαῖόν τι φέρειν αὐτόν, εἰς μέσον τὴν σκάφην προήγαγον. ἔτυχε δέ τις παρὼν ἐκεῖ τῶν τὰ παιδάρια ἐκθεμένων· ὃς τὴν σκάφην γνωρίσας, δραμὼν φράζει τῷ Ἀμουλίῳ. καὶ ὁ Φαυστοῦλος ἀνακρινόμενος παρὰ τοῦ βασιλέως σώζεσθαι μὲν τοὺς παῖδας κατέθετο, πόρρω δὲ τῆς Ἄλβης νέμοντας εἶναι· τὴν δὲ σκάφην πρὸς τὴν Ἰλίαν κομίζειν τὴν τῶν παίδων μητέρα, ποθοῦσαν ἰδεῖν. τεταραγμένος δὲ τούτοις Ἀμούλιος ἄνδρα πρὸς τὸν Νομίτωρα πέπομφε πυνθανόμενος εἴ τι μάθοι περὶ τῶν παίδων ὡς περιόντων. ἦν δὲ τῶν φίλων ὁ πεμφθεὶς τοῦ Νομίτωρος. ἀπελθὼν οὖν καὶ ἐν περιπλοκαῖς τοῦ Ῥώμου εὑρηκὼς τὸν Νομίτωρα, παρεθάρρυνέ τε καὶ μὴ μέλλειν αὐτοῖς συνεβούλευε, καὶ αὐτὸς δὲ συνέπραττεν. ἄρτι δὲ καὶ ὁ Ῥωμύλος ἐγγὺς ἦν, χεῖρα συχνὴν ἀγροικικὴν ἐπαγόμενος· καὶ τῶν πολιτῶν δὲ αὐτῷ οὐκ ὀλίγοι προσῆσαν μίσει τοῦ Ἀμουλίου. ὃς οὕτω τῶν πραγμάτων συνενεχθέντων οὐδὲν οὔτε πράξας οὔτε βουλεύσας σωτήριον ἀνῃρέθη.

7.3

The Founding of Rome

Romulus and Remus then gave the throne to their maternal grandfather Numitor, and to their mother they gave an honor which they judged suitable to themselves. For they did not undertake to seize power, and moreover they wished to found a city on the spot where they were nursed. When they set about the task of building the new city, there arose between the brothers a dispute about the city and who would be sovereign, and it came to blows; in this contest, Remus died. Another story has it that as Romulus was digging a trench which was to be the city enclosure, Remus now hindered the work, and now scoffed at it. At last, when Remus leapt over it as if to show how easily it could be attacked, he was killed; some say that this was at Romulus' hands, and others aver that he was slain by some other man. For this reason, it was enacted that anyone who dared to cross the trench except by the customary paths would be condemned to death.

After burying his brother, Romulus settled his city. He yoked a bull to a cow and threw a bronze ploughshare onto the plough; he then dug a large circular furrow, and those who followed him took the clods of earth which the plough dug out and turned them all around the furrow. Once it was time for the wall to be constructed, as it was said, the furrow was dug up where they had contrived to erect the walls, and they made intervals in the furrow, by lifting the plough up above them. For, they consider every wall a sacred thing; but if they had considered the gates sacred, it would not have been possible to bring in and send out some of the necessary and even impure articles of life.

The founding of the city was completed on the eleventh day

7.3
Ἡ Κτίσις τῆς Ῥώμης

Ῥωμύλος μέντοι καὶ Ῥῶμος τὴν τῆς Ἄλβης ἡγεμονίαν τῷ μητροπάτορι νείμαντες, καὶ τῇ μητρὶ τιμὴν πρέπουσαν, καθ' ἑαυτοὺς εἶναι ἔκριναν· οὔτε γὰρ ἠνείχοντο ἄρχεσθαι καὶ πόλιν ἀναστῆσαι ἔνθα προετράφησαν ἤθελον. ὡρμημένοις δὲ πρὸς τὴν τῆς πόλεως δόμησιν διαφορὰ συνέβη τοῖς ἀδελφοῖς περί τε τῆς ἀρχῆς καὶ περὶ τῆς πόλεως, καὶ διὰ μάχης ἐχώρησαν, ἐν ᾗ ὁ Ῥῶμος ἀπέθανεν. ἕτερος δὲ λόγος ἔχει ὡς τοῦ Ῥωμύλου τάφρον ἤδη ὀρύττοντος, ἣ τῆς πόλεως ἔμελλεν εἶναι προτείχισμα, πῇ μὲν ἀπεῖργε τὸ ἔργον ὁ Ῥῶμος, πῇ δέ γε ἐχλεύαζε· καὶ τέλος διαλλόμενον αὐτὴν ὡς εὐεπιχείρητον οἱ μὲν Ῥωμύλου πατάξαντος, οἱ δ' ἑτέρου τινὸς ἱστοροῦσι πεσεῖν. ὅθεν καὶ ἐνομίσθη τὸν στρατοπέδου τάφρον τολμήσαντα διελθεῖν παρὰ τὰς συνήθεις ὁδούς, θανατοῦσθαι.

Ὁ δὲ Ῥωμύλος θάψας τὸν ἀδελφὸν ᾤκιζε τὴν πόλιν καὶ βοῦν ἄρρενα συζεύξας θηλείᾳ, καὶ ἀρότρῳ ὕννιν χαλκῆν ἐμβαλών, αὐτὸς μὲν αὔλακα βαθεῖαν κυκλοτερῆ περιέγραψεν, οἱ δ' ἑπόμενοι τὰς βώλους, ἃς ἀνίστη τὸ ἄροτρον, εἴσω πάσας τῆς αὔλακος περιέστρεφον. καὶ ὅπου μὲν ἔμελλε τὸ τεῖχος ἀνίστασθαι, καθὼς εἴρηται, ἡ αὖλαξ ἐτέτμητο, ἔνθα δὲ πύλας στῆσαι διενοοῦντο, διάλειμμα ἐποιοῦντο τῆς αὔλακος, τὸ ἄροτρον ἀνέχοντες ὕπερθεν. πᾶν μὲν γὰρ τεῖχος νομίζουσιν ἱερόν· τὰς δὲ πύλας εἴπερ ἥγηντο ἱεράς, οὐκ ἦν τὰ μὲν δι' αὐτῶν εἰσάγειν, τὰ δὲ ἀποπέμπειν τῶν ἀναγκαίων καὶ μὴ καθαρῶν.

Ἡ δὲ κτίσις τῆς πόλεως ταύτης ἡμέρᾳ τετέλεστο τῇ πρὸ ἕνδεκα καλανδῶν Μαΐων, ἢ ἂν εἴη μᾶλλον εἰκοστῇ Ἀπριλλίου

before the Kalends of May, or better perhaps, on the twentieth of April. The Romans celebrate that day with festivals,

Now that the city was founded, he rounded up as much of the mob was the right age for military service and drew them up into military contingents. Each of these contingents consisted of three thousand infantry and three hundred cavalry, and was called a legion, because the fighters were chosen from all, while all of the rest were proclaimed part of the citizen body, which they named the people *(populus)*. For this reason in their law books the assembly of the people is called the "popular" *(populāria)* assembly. He then marked out as counselors a hundred of the men most prominent for their birth, prudence, and mode of life, and called them patricians. The rest of the organized government he called the senate, which is the counsel of old men *(gerousía)*. The patricians were so called either because they were the fathers of legitimate offspring, or perhaps more likely because they were able to demonstrate that their fathers were descended from well-known families, or from their *patrōnia.* (Thus they called the relationship of patronage, for they called those who took care of and protected a person "patrons.") One could readily guess at Romulus' motive here: he thought that by this appellation, it would be clear that the chief and most powerful men of the state would need to employ a certain paternal care for the lowborn, and that simultaneously the common people would be led on by the name of "patricians" not to feel put-upon by the honors granted to those more powerful than them, but would rather submit to it peacefully by both calling and considering them as "fathers."

There were now many men living in the city, of whom very few were wedded to wives. So, Romulus had the idea that they could unite women to themselves. For they were just a mob who had come from difficult and undistinguished circumstances, and they were despised in their marriage suits by all of the

καὶ τὴν ἡμέραν ταύτην ἑορτάζουσι Ῥωμαῖοι, γενέθλιον τῆς πατρίδος ὀνομάζοντες. ὀκτωκαίδεκα δ' εἶναι Ῥωμύλος ἐνιαυτῶν ἀναγέγραπται ὅτε τὴν Ῥώμην συνῴκισεν. ἔκτισε δὲ αὐτὴν περὶ τὴν τοῦ Φαυστούλου οἴκησιν· ὠνόμαστο δ' ὁ χῶρος Παλάτιον.

Κτισθείσης μέντοι τῆς πόλεως, ὅσον μὲν ἐν ἡλικίᾳ στρατευσίμῳ πλῆθος ἐτύγχανεν, εἰς στρατιωτικὰ διεῖλε συντάγματα, ἕκαστον δὲ σύνταγμα πεζῶν τρισχιλίων ἦν καὶ τριακοσίων ἱππέων, ἐκλήθη δὲ λεγεών, ὅτι λογάδες ἦσαν ἐκ πάντων οἱ μάχιμοι, τοῖς δ' ἄλλοις δήμῳ ἐκέχρητο. καὶ τὸν δῆμον ποπούλους ὠνόμασεν· ὅθεν καὶ παρὰ ταῖς βίβλοις ταῖς νομικαῖς ποπουλαρία κέκληται ἡ δημοτικὴ ἀγωγή. τῶν μέντοι περιφανεστέρων γένει τε καὶ συνέσει καὶ βίου αἱρέσει ἑκατὸν ἀπέδειξε βουλευτάς, πατρικίους ὀνομάσας αὐτούς· τὸ δὲ λοιπὸν σύστημα σενᾶτον προσηγόρευσεν, ὅ ἐστι γερουσία. πατρίκιοι μέντοι οἱ βουλευταὶ ἐπεκλήθησαν ἢ ὅτι παίδων ἦσαν γνησίων πατέρες, ἢ μᾶλλον ὅτι αὐτοὶ πατέρας ἑαυτῶν ἀποδεικνύειν ἠδύναντο ἕκαστος ἐκ γένους ὄντες γνωρίμου, ἢ ἀπὸ τῆς πατρωνίας· οὕτω δ' ἐκάλουν τὴν προστασίαν· πάτρωνας γὰρ τοὺς κηδεμονικοὺς καὶ βοηθητικοὺς προσηγόρευον. μάλιστα δ' ἄν τις καταστοχάσαιτο τῆς τοῦ Ῥωμύλου διανοίας, εἰ οἴοιτο διὰ τῆς κλήσεως ταύτης ἐμφαίνειν χρῆναι τοὺς πρώτους καὶ δυνατωτάτους τῆς πόλεως πατρικῇ κηδεμονίᾳ κήδεσθαι τῶν ταπεινοτέρων, ἅμα δὲ καὶ τὸν δῆμον ἐνάγειν διὰ τῆς τῶν πατρικίων προσηγορίας εἰς τὸ μὴ ἄχθεσθαι ταῖς τῶν κρειττόνων τιμαῖς, ἀλλ' εὐνοϊκῶς διακεῖσθαι, νομίζοντας πατέρας αὐτοὺς καὶ προσαγορεύοντας.

Πολλῶν δὲ τῇ πόλει ἐνοικισθέντων, ὧν ὀλίγοι γυναιξὶ συνεζεύγνυντο, φροντὶς τῷ Ῥωμύλῳ ἐγένετο ἵνα κἀκεῖνοι γυναῖκας ἑαυτοῖς συνοικίσωσι. σύγκλυδες γὰρ καὶ ἐξ ἀπόρων ὄντες καὶ ἀφανῶν, ὑπερωρῶντο πρὸς κῆδος παρὰ τῶν

neighboring tribes. Romulus then planned for his citizens to take wives by means of forcible seizure, so he announced that there would be a sacrifice, some games, and a religious assembly on the pretext that a strange new altar of the gods had been discovered. Many people came together for this. Romulus himself, however, sat at the front among the nobles, outfitted in a purple robe. He gave as the sign that the undertaking should commence the sudden spreading and re-fastening of his robe. Once this sign was given, the men, grabbing their swords, set out and grabbed the maiden daughters of the Sabines – not, indeed, anyone's wife.

Once this violence had been dared, the Sabines, being a numerous and warlike race who dwelled in un-walled villages on account of their lofty spirit (as if they were a colony of Spartans), sent an embassy to Romulus and demanded that the Romans leave off the work of violence, and instead work toward friendship and neighborliness with the nearby people under the influence of reason and law. When Romulus refused to send the maidens back, and demanded that the Sabines accept their new relationship, some of them wasted their time in planning, but Akron, the high-spirited and warlike king of the Caeneniti, rose up and with a considerable force set out against Romulus. When they came against each other, they called on one another to commit the battle while both armies remained stationary. There was then a single combat between Romulus and Acron, in which Romulus threw down Acron, and also routed his army when the battle began. He then took their city, but did not mete out any punishment to them, but simply ordered them to destroy their houses and follow him to Rome, where they would become citizens and receive equal treatment.

Thereupon some of the Sabines fought with the Romans and were defeated. The rest of the Sabines made Titus Tatius their leader and set out against Rome. They took the Capitoline, which was

γειτνιώντων ἐθνῶν. βουλεύεται τοίνυν ἐξ ἁρπαγῆς λαβεῖν γυναῖκας τοὺς πολίτας αὐτοῦ, καὶ κηρύσσει θυσίαν καὶ ἀγῶνα καὶ θέαν μέλλειν τελεῖν πανηγυρικήν, ὡς βωμοῦ εὑρημένου θεοῦ καινοῦ. καὶ πολλοὶ συνῆλθον. αὐτὸς δὲ προυκάθητο μετὰ τῶν ἀρίστων, ἁλουργίδι κεκοσμημένος· δέδωκε δὲ τῷ δήμῳ τῆς ἐπιχειρήσεως σύμβολον τὴν τῆς ἁλουργίδος διάπτυξιν καὶ αὖθις ταύτης περιβολήν. οὗ γενομένου σπασάμενοι τὰ ξίφη μετὰ βοῆς ὥρμησαν καὶ ἥρπαζον τὰς θυγατέρας τῶν Σαβίνων παρθένους, οὐ μέντοι γυναῖκάς τινων.

Τολμηθείσης δὲ τῆς ἁρπαγῆς οἱ Σαβῖνοι, πολλοὶ καὶ πολεμικοὶ ὄντες καὶ κώμας ἀτειχίστους οἰκοῦντες διὰ τὸ μέγα φρονεῖν ὡς Λακεδαιμονίων ἄποικοι, πρεσβείαν πρὸς τὸν Ῥωμύλον πεποίηνται, λῦσαι τὸ τῆς βίας ἔργον ζητοῦντες, πειθοῖ δὲ καὶ νόμῳ πράττειν τοῖς γένεσι φιλίαν καὶ οἰκειότητα. τοῦ δὲ Ῥωμύλου τὰς μὲν κόρας μὴ προϊεμένου, ἀξιοῦντος δὲ τὴν κοινωνίαν δέχεσθαι τοὺς Σαβίνους, οἱ μὲν ἄλλοι βουλευόμενοι διέτριβον, Ἄκρων δὲ ὁ βασιλεὺς τῶν Καινηνιτῶν, θυμοειδὴς ἀνὴρ καὶ πολεμικώτατος, προεξανέστη καὶ μετὰ πολλῆς ἐχώρει δυνάμεως ἐπὶ τὸν Ῥωμύλον. ὁμοῦ δὲ γεγονότες ἀλλήλους προυκαλοῦντο μάχεσθαι, ἀτρεμούντων τῶν στρατευμάτων. τῆς γοῦν μονομαχίας ἀμφοῖν γενομένης καταβάλλει μὲν ὁ Ῥωμύλος τὸν Ἄκρωνα, τρέπεται δὲ καὶ τὸ ἐκείνου στράτευμα μάχης συγκροτηθείσης· καὶ τὴν πόλιν αἱρεῖ, οὐ μέντοι τοὺς ἐν αὐτῇ κακόν τι διέθετο, ἀλλ' ἢ μόνον ἐκέλευσε τὰς οἰκίας καθελόντας ἀκολουθεῖν εἰς Ῥώμην αὐτῷ, ὡς πολίτας ἐσομένους καὶ τῶν ἴσων ἀξιωθησομένους.

Εἶτα καὶ ἄλλοι τῶν Σαβίνων τοῖς Ῥωμαίοις ἐμαχέσαντο καὶ ἡττήθησαν. ἐπὶ τούτοις οἱ λοιποὶ τῶν Σαβίνων στρατηγὸν τὸν Τάτιον ἀποδείξαντες ἐπὶ τὴν Ῥώμην ἐστράτευσαν καὶ τὸ Καπιτώλιον εἷλον προδεδομένον

betrayed by Tarpeia, the daughter of the Roman general. For she went down to the water where she was caught and brought to Titus Tatius, and she was persuaded to betray the defense of the city because she was desirous of the golden bracelets, which the Sabines were wearing on their left arms. She demanded these bracelets as a payment for her betrayal. At night, when Tatius had taken his position, she opened one gate and let the Sabines in. As Tatius entered, he commanded his forces to give Tarpeia whatever they had on their left arms. Tatius was the first to toss his armlet at Tarpeia, along with his shield. When everyone else did likewise, she was struck with the gold and, being showered with shields, she died under their weighty multitude.

This man Tatius accomplished in deed what Caesar and Antigonus subsequently talked about with words. For he claimed that he loved treachery but hated the traitor. Antigonus, however, said that he would welcome those who were in the act of treachery, but decreed death to those who had completed their treason.

ὑπὸ Ταρπηίας τῆς θυγατρὸς τοῦ φρουράρχου. ἐκείνη γὰρ ἐφ' ὕδωρ κατελθοῦσα συνελήφθη καὶ ἤχθη πρὸς Τάτιον, καὶ ἀνεπείσθη προδοῦναι τὸ ἔρυμα, τῶν χρυσῶν βραχιονιστήρων ἐρασθεῖσα, οὓς ἐν ταῖς ἀριστεραῖς ἐφόρουν χερσὶν οἱ Σαβῖνοι, καὶ μισθὸν ὑπὲρ τῆς προδοσίας λαβεῖν αὐτοὺς ἀπαιτήσασα. συνθεμένου δὲ τοῦ Τατίου νύκτωρ μίαν πύλην ἀνοίξασα τοὺς Σαβίνους ἐδέξατο. εἰσελθὼν δὲ ὁ Τάτιος ἐκέλευσε τοὺς ὑπ' αὐτὸν ὅσα ἐν ταῖς ἀριστεραῖς χερσὶν ἔφερον διδόναι αὐτῇ, καὶ πρῶτος αὐτὸς τὸν βραχιονιστῆρα τῇ Ταρπηίᾳ ἐπέρριψε καὶ τὸν θυρεόν. πάντων δὲ ὁμοίως ποιούντων βαλλομένη τε τῷ χρυσῷ καὶ καταχωσθεῖσα τοῖς θυρεοῖς ὑπὸ πλήθους καὶ βάρους ἀπέθανεν.

Ἔργῳ οὖν οὗτος ἐποίησεν ὃ λόγοις ὕστερον εἶπον ὁ Καῖσαρ καὶ ὁ Ἀντίγονος· ὁ μὲν γὰρ προδοσίαν ἔφη φιλεῖν, προδότην δὲ μισεῖν· ὁ δὲ Ἀντίγονος προδιδόντας μὲν ἀσπασίως εἶπε προσίεσθαι, προδεδωκόσι δὲ ἀπεχθάνεσθαι.

7.4

The Reign of Romulus

When the heights had been abandoned by the Sabines, fierce fighting broke out between them and the Romans, in which many people were slain, and Romulus was struck on the head with a rock. The captive daughters checked their Sabine kinsmen who were still prepared to fight, and were seen shouting here and wailing there. They brought out their babies in their arms, they loosed their hair, and they called now upon the Sabines, and now upon the Romans, with various terms of endearment. The enemies were moved to pity and stood apart while the women stood in the middle of the lines, and all sides began to cry. Once the women had made their point, the opposing leaders made a parley, and the women who so wished were allowed to remain with the men who now possessed them, with an exemption from every deed and all daily work except for spinning wool. Furthermore, the Romans and Sabines would jointly inhabit the city, which was to be called Rome after Romulus, but the citizens were to be named Kurites (Quirites) after Kurita, the father of Titus Tatius. Both peoples would rule the city, and they would marshal armies jointly. The place in which they made this agreement was called the Comitium, clearly because it was a spot for meeting, because among the Romans the word *comīre* means to come together. Moreover, another hundred men were selected from the Sabines and added to the number of patricians. At first, the kings did not take counsel in common among each other, but in private with their own hundred patricians. Subsequently, all came together in the same place.

In the fifth year of Tatius' joint reign with Romulus, some of his kinsmen encountered some elders walking along the road from

7.4
Ἡ Ἀρχὴ τοῦ Ῥωμύλου

Ληφθείσης δὲ τῆς ἄκρας ὑπὸ τῶν Σαβίνων, μάχη καρτερὰ συνερράγη μέσον αὐτῶν καὶ Ῥωμαίων, ἐν ᾗ πολλοὶ μὲν ἔπεσον, ὁ δὲ Ῥωμύλος ἐπλήγη λίθῳ τὴν κεφαλήν. ἔτι δὲ μάχεσθαι παρασκευαζομένους τοὺς Σαβίνους ἐπέσχον αἱ ἡρπασμέναι θυγατέρες αὐτῶν, ἄλλοθεν ἄλλαι μετὰ βοῆς καὶ ὀλολυγμοῦ ὀφθεῖσαι αὐτοῖς, αἱ μὲν νήπια πρὸς ταῖς ἀγκάλαις κομίζουσαι, αἱ δὲ τὴν κόμην προϊσχόμεναι λελυμένην, πᾶσαι δὲ ἀνακαλούμεναι τοῖς φιλτάτοις ὀνόμασι ποτὲ μὲν τοὺς Σαβίνους, ποτὲ δὲ τοὺς Ῥωμαίους. ἐπεκλάσθησαν οὖν οἱ ἐναντίοι καὶ διέστησαν αὐταῖς ἐν μέσῳ στῆναι τῆς παρατάξεως, καὶ κλαυθμὸς ἅμα διὰ πάντων ἐχώρει. διαλεχθέντων δὲ τῶν γυναίων συνῆλθον εἰς λόγους οἱ ἡγεμόνες καὶ συνέθεντο τῶν μὲν γυναικῶν αἳ βούλονται τοῖς ἔχουσι συνοικεῖν, παντὸς ἔργου καὶ πάσης λατρείας πλὴν ταλασίας ἀφειμένας, οἰκεῖν δὲ τὴν πόλιν Ῥωμαίους καὶ Σαβίνους κοινῇ, καὶ καλεῖσθαι αὐτὴν Ῥώμην ἐπὶ Ῥωμύλῳ, Κυρίτας δὲ Ῥωμαίους ἐπὶ τῇ Τατίου πατρίδι Κυρίτα, βασιλεύειν δὲ κοινῇ καὶ στρατηγεῖν ἀμφοτέρους. ὁ δὲ τόπος ἐν ᾧ τὰς συνθήκας ἔθεντο καλεῖται κομίτιον, τόπος δηλαδὴ συνελεύσεως· κόμιρε γὰρ Ῥωμαίοις τὸ συνελθεῖν λέγεται. προσκατελέχθησαν δὲ τοῖς πατρικίοις ἐκ τῶν Σαβίνων ἕτεροι ἑκατόν. ἐβουλεύοντο δὲ οἱ βασιλεῖς οὐκ εὐθὺς ἐν κοινῷ μετ' ἀλλήλων, ἀλλ' ἑκάτερος πρότερον ἰδίᾳ μετὰ τῶν ἑκατόν· εἶτα εἰς τὸ αὐτὸ πάντες συνήγοντο.

Ἔτει δὲ πέμπτῳ τοῦ Τατίου Ῥωμύλῳ συμβασιλεύοντος συγγενεῖς αὐτοῦ πρέσβεσι καθ' ὁδὸν ἐντυχόντες εἰς Ῥώμην ἀπὸ

23

Larentum to Rome, and attempted to take from them by force the goods but rather attempted to protect them, they were killed by Tatius' men. Romulus then cast his vote to chastise the men who had committed this injustice, but Tatius opposed him and tried to lead him away from his purpose. This alone was the cause of the manifest rupture in their friendship. Since the kinsmen of those who were killed did not receive justice, they set upon Tatius as he was making sacrifice in the Alban Hills and killed him. They sent Romulus away with some well-wishing because they considered him a just man. The murder of Titus Tatius did not disturb the Sabines; some of them were well-disposed to Romulus, and others continued to yield to him out of fear for his power. Thereupon, a plague fell upon the city, bringing much sudden death to its inhabitants without any illness; there was moreover a lack of grain, and all of the herds and flocks became sterile. Drops of blood even rained on the city. Similar things happened in Laurentum. It seemed that a heaven-sent fury pursued these cities on account of the murder of Tatius and those ambassadors who had been killed by the Sabines. When they gave up the murderers and punished them, the terrible portents ceased.

While things were going well for the Romans, those with less power stooped under the yoke of their neighbors, while the powerful did not think that it was necessary to take this into consideration, but rather to check their growth. The people of Veii were the first of the Tyrrhenians to start a war against Rome. They came against the Romans and, losing many men, the made a treaty of friendship lasting one hundred years, and they offered fifty of their noblest citizens as hostages.

Romulus led those whom he had conquered in triumph. Then, puffed up by his own unbelievable good fortune and being possessed of a rather dull mind, he departed from the more democratic aspects of government and exchanged it for a burdensome and grievous form

Λαυρεντοῦ βαδίζουσιν ἐπεχείρουν ἀφαιρεῖσθαι βίᾳ τὰ χρήματα ἃ ἐπήγοντο, καὶ μὴ προϊεμένους, ἀλλ' ἀμυνομένους ἀνεῖλον. ὁ μὲν οὖν Ῥωμύλος κολάζεσθαι τοὺς ἀδικήσαντας ἐψηφίζετο, ὁ δὲ Τάτιος ἐξέκρουε καὶ παρῆγε· καὶ τοῦτο μόνον ὑπῆρξεν αἴτιον σφίσι διαφορᾶς ἐμφανοῦς. οἱ δὲ τῶν ἀνηρημένων οἰκεῖοι μὴ τυγχάνοντες δίκης, ἐν Ἀλβανῷ θύοντα μετὰ Ῥωμύλου τὸν Τάτιον προσπεσόντες κτιννύουσι· τὸν δὲ Ῥωμύλον ὡς δίκαιον ἄνδρα σὺν εὐφημίαις προέπεμψαν. οὐ μὴν ἐτάραξε τοὺς Σαβίνους ὁ φόνος τοῦ σφῶν ἄρχοντος, ἀλλ' οἱ μὲν εὐνοίᾳ τῇ πρὸς Ῥωμύλον, οἱ δὲ φόβῳ τῆς δυνάμεως εἴκοντες διετέλουν. εἶτα λοιμὸς ἐμπίπτει τῇ πόλει θανάτους αἰφνιδίους ἀνθρώποις ἐπιφέρων νόσων χωρίς, καὶ ἀφορία καρπῶν καὶ θρεμμάτων ἀγονία ὕσθη δὲ καὶ σταγόσιν αἵματος ἡ πόλις. ὅμοια δὲ καὶ τοῖς Λαυρεντίοις συνέβαινεν. ἐδόκει τοίνυν διὰ τὸν Τατίου φόνον καὶ τοὺς παρὰ τῶν Σαβίνων ἀνῃρημένους πρέσβεις ποινηλατεῖν τὰς πόλεις δαιμόνιον μήνιμα. ἐκδοθέντων δὲ τῶν φονέων καὶ κολασθέντων ἐλώφησαν τὰ δεινά.

Ῥωννυμένων δὲ τῶν πραγμάτων Ῥωμαίοις οἱ μὲν ἀσθενέστεροι τῶν προσοίκων ὑπέκυπτον, οἱ δυνατοὶ δὲ οὐκ ᾤοντο δεῖν περιορᾶν, ἀλλὰ κολούειν τὴν αὔξησιν. πρῶτοι δὲ Τυρρηνῶν Οὔιοι ἀρχὴν ἐποιήσαντο πολέμου. συμβαλόντες οὖν καὶ πολλοὺς ἀποβαλόντες ὁμολογίαν ἐποιήσαντο καὶ φιλίαν ἐπὶ ἐνιαυτοὺς ἑκατόν, καὶ τῶν παρ' αὐτοῖς ἀρίστων παρέσχον εἰς ὁμηρείαν πεντήκοντα.

Ἐθριάμβευσεν οὖν τούτους νικήσας Ῥωμύλος. εἶτα ἐπαρθεὶς ταῖς παραλόγοις εὐτυχίαις καὶ βαρυτέρῳ φρονήματι χρώμενος ἐξίστατο τοῦ δημοτικοῦ καὶ παρήλλαττε καὶ εἰς ἐπαχθῆ μοναρχίαν καὶ λυποῦσαν ἀπὸ τοῦ σχήματος ἑαυτὸν ἐσχημάτιζεν. ἁλουργῆ μὲν γὰρ ἐνεδύετο χιτῶνα καὶ τήβεννον

of monarchy which he fashioned after his own mold. He then began to wear a purple cloak, as well a toga encircled with purple, red sandals, and he delivered his declarations while sitting in a reclining chair. There were always about his person many young men, whom he called 'Celeres,' which in the language of the Romans means 'swift,' and some others walked before him bearing rods which they used to part the crowd, and they had straps tied to them, so that they could bind those whom they ordered around.

When Romulus' grandfather Numitor died in Alba Longa and the throne of that city fell to Romulus, he led some people to found a city between Alba Longa and Rome, and every year he produced a new leader for the Sabines. He grew angry at the powerful in Rome who sought an autonomous city without a king. For, those who were called 'Patricians' did not have a part in the city's affairs, but rather a title and the outward appearance of power; they were brought together in the senate house more for the sake of custom than for the sake of their counsel. Then, while Romulus was in action, they would listen in silence, and they considered it better to learn what seemed better to him than to consult the opinion of the other, so they ignored the rest. From this circumstance arose the opinion that he treated the senate with indignity. On that account, it seemed suspicious when Romulus suddenly disappeared. It is said that while he was calling an assembly in the spot known as the Goat's Meadow the sun lost its light, night descended upon everything, and there was terrible thunder along with gusts of wind which brought driving rain. In this storm, the masses fled, but the powerful men took shelter with each other. When the storm had subsided, and they had come together again, they began to seek the king. The powerful men did not allow anyone to inquire after Romulus, but ordered everyone to respect him and worship him, as he had been snatched away to be with the gods, and he would be a god to the Romans in place of a simple king.

ἠμπίσχετο περιπόρφυρον καὶ πεδίλοις ἐκέχρητο ἐρυθροῖς καὶ ἐν θρόνῳ ἀνακλίτῳ καθήμενος ἐχρημάτιζεν· ἦσαν δὲ περὶ αὐτὸν ἀεὶ καὶ τῶν νέων συχνοί, οὓς Κέλερας προσηγόρευεν, ὃ κατὰ τὴν τῶν Ῥωμαίων διάλεκτον δηλοῖ τοὺς ταχεῖς, καὶ πρόσθεν ἐβάδιζον ἕτεροι βακτηρίαις τὸν ὄχλον ἀνείργοντες, ὑπεζωσμένοι ἱμάντας, ὥστε συνδεῖν οὓς κελευσθῶσιν.

Ἐπεὶ δὲ Νομίτωρος τοῦ πάππου αὐτοῦ ἐν Ἄλβῃ τελευτήσαντος, Ῥωμύλῳ προσηκούσης τῆς βασιλείας, αὐτὸς εἰς μέσον ἔθηκε τὴν πολιτείαν δημαγωγῶν, καὶ κατ' ἐνιαυτὸν ἀπεδείκνυεν ἄρχοντα τοῖς Σαβίνοις, ἠρέθισε τοὺς ἐν Ῥώμῃ δυνατοὺς ἀβασίλευτον ζητεῖν καὶ αὐτόνομον πολιτείαν. οὐδὲ γὰρ οἱ καλούμενοι πατρίκιοι πραγμάτων μετεῖχον, ἀλλ' ὄνομα καὶ σχῆμα ἦν αὐτοῖς, ἔθους ἕνεκα μᾶλλον ἢ γνώμης ἀθροιζομένοις εἰς τὸ βουλευτήριον εἶτα Ῥωμύλου πράττοντος ἠκροῶντο σιγῇ, καὶ τὸ πρὸ τῶν ἄλλων τὸ δεδογμένον ἐκείνῳ μαθεῖν πλέον ἔχοντες τῶν λοιπῶν ἀπηλλάττοντο. ὅθεν ἐδόκει τὴν γερουσίαν προπηλακίζειν διὸ αὕτη ὕποπτος ἔδοξεν ἀφανοῦς μετ' ὀλίγον γενομένου Ῥωμύλου. λέγεται γὰρ ἐκκλησίαν ἄγοντος αὐτοῦ περὶ τὸ καλούμενον Αἰγὸς ἕλος τοῦ μὲν ἡλίου τὸ φῶς ἐπιλιπεῖν, νύκτα δὲ κατασχεῖν βροντάς τε δεινὰς συμβῆναι καὶ πνοὰς ἀνέμων ζάλην ἐλαυνούσας. ἐν δὲ τούτῳ τὸν μὲν ὄχλον φεύγειν, τοὺς δὲ δυνατοὺς συστραφῆναι μετ' ἀλλήλων. τῆς δ' ἐν τῷ ἀέρι ταραχῆς λωφησάσης καὶ αὖθις πολλῶν ὁμοῦ γενομένων ζητεῖσθαι τὸν βασιλέα· τοὺς δὲ δυνατοὺς οὐκ ἐᾶν ἐξετάζειν περὶ αὐτοῦ, τιμᾶν δὲ παρακελεύεσθαι πᾶσι καὶ σέβεσθαι Ῥωμύλον ὡς ἀνηρπασμένον εἰς θεούς, καὶ θεὸν ἐσόμενον σφίσιν ἀντὶ χρηστοῦ βασιλέως.

Many, being captivated by these salutary hopes, believed the account of Romulus' disappearance. Some, however, felt suspicious of the patricians and were afraid that they were trying to snow the citizens with a stupid storywhen they were in actual fact themselves the murderers of Romulus. They would have offered resisitance to the patricians if it were not for Julius Proculus, a man distinguished for his birth, excellent in character, and a close friend of Romulus. Proculus came to the forum and swore under oath that Romulus appeared to him, big and beautiful as never before, and decked out with shining, even flaming, arms; he claimed that he asked Romulus, 'Suffering what, O King, have you left us to these toilsome squabbles, and the whole city in grief?' Romulus responded, 'It seemed to the gods, O Proculus, that I had spent enough time among mortals, and that I should dwell again in the heavens, where I now am. But take heart and tell the Romans that if they stay wise and manly, they will achieve the height of human power. I, Quirinus, will forever be well-disposed to you all.' All of this seemed believable to the Romans because of the speaker's oath and general character; no one spoke out against this account, and setting aside all suspicion and plotting they prayed to and worshipped Quirinus. They say that Romulus acquired this name either because they called some of the citizens Quirites or because the ancients called either spear-points or spear-shafts *quirītēs*. Thus they called Romulus, braver than a warrior god, Quirinus. It was said that he lived fifty-four years, and that he disappeared in the thirty-eighth year of his reign.

Οἱ μὲν οὖν πολλοὶ πεπεισμένοι τοῖς λόγοις ἀπηλλάττοντο ἐλπίσι χρησταῖς αἰωρούμενοι, ἔνιοι δὲ ἐν ὑπονοίαις τοὺς πατρικίους πεποίηντο καὶ ἐτάραττον ὡς τὸν δῆμον ἀβέλτερα πείθοντας, αὐτοὺς τοῦ βασιλέως γεγονότας αὐτόχειρας. καὶ πράγματα ἂν παρέσχον τοῖς δυνατοῖς, εἰ μή τις τῶν ἱππέων Ἰούλιος Πρόκλος, γένει τε δοκιμώτατος καὶ ἤθει χρηστὸς καὶ Ῥωμύλῳ πιστός, εἰς ἀγορὰν ἐλθὼν ἐνόρκως εἶπεν ὡς ὀφθείη Ῥωμύλος αὐτῷ καλὸς καὶ μέγας ὡς οὔποτε πρόσθεν καὶ ὅπλοις λαμπροῖς κεκοσμημένος καὶ φλέγουσι, καὶ ὡς αὐτὸς μὲν πύθοιτο "τί δὴ παθών, ὦ βασιλεῦ, ἡμᾶς μὲν ἐν αἰτίαις πεποίηκας πονηραῖς, πᾶσαν δὲ τὴν πόλιν ἐν πένθει προλέλοιπας;" ἐκεῖνος δὲ πρὸς ταῦτα ἀμείψαιτο "θεοῖς ἔδοξεν, ὦ Πρόκλε, τοσοῦτον ἡμᾶς μετ' ἀνθρώπων γενέσθαι χρόνον, αὖθις δ' οὐρανὸν οἰκεῖν, ἐκεῖθεν ὄντας. ἀλλὰ χαῖρε καὶ φράζε Ῥωμαίοις ὅτι σωφροσύνην καὶ ἀνδρείαν ἀσκοῦντες ἐπὶ πλεῖστον δυνάμεως ἀνθρωπίνης ἀφίξονται. ἐγὼ δὲ ὑμῖν εὐμενὴς ἔσομαι Κυρῖνος." ταῦτα διά τε τὸν ὅρκον τοῦ λέγοντος καὶ τὸν τρόπον πιστὰ Ῥωμαίοις ἐδόκει τοσοῦτον ὡς μή τινα ἀντειπεῖν, πάσης δὲ ἀφεμένους ὑποψίας τε καὶ διαβολῆς εὔχεσθαι Κυρίνῳ καὶ θεοκλυτεῖν. ταύτην δὲ τὴν ἐπωνυμίαν φασὶ τῷ Ῥωμύλῳ γενέσθαι ἢ ὅτι τοὺς πολίτας Κυρίτας ὠνόμαζον ἢ ὅτι τὴν αἰχμὴν ἢ τὸ δόρυ κυρῖνον ἐκάλουν οἱ παλαιοί· ὡς οὖν ἀρήιόν τινα τὸν Ῥωμύλον ἢ αἰχμητὴν θεὸν ὀνομασθῆναι Κυρῖνον. λέγεται δὲ τέσσαρα μὲν ἔτη καὶ πεντήκοντα βιῶναι, ὄγδοον δ' ἐπὶ τριακοστῷ βασιλεύων ἐνιαυτὸν ἐξ ἀνθρώπων ἀφανισθῆναι.

The Reign of Numa Pompilius

Once all of this had happened regarding Romulus, it seemed right to everyone that there should continue to be a monarchy, but strife and discord arose among those in Rome not just about who, individually, should be the king, but about whether he should be Roman or Sabine. To those first men who founded the city with Romulus, it seemed unbearable that the Sabines, who had come to the city after them, should take it in hand to rule. The Sabines thought, on the contrary, that since Romulus ruled by himself after the death of Titus Tatius, it was right that the new king should be selected from among themselves.

Both parties thus contended against each other. Since the state was held in suspense on this matter, the Patricians, being then 150 in number, established that each one of them would, in turns, dress himself in the royal outfit and both sacrifice to the gods and give orders to the state for six hours of the night and six hours of the day. This apportionment of parts equally among each patrician seemed to hold up well, even to the citizens who were ruled by the system. The rapid exchange of power tended to dispel enmity, since even subjects could see that the same day and night elevated a man from a private station to regal dignity, and then returned him to private life. I know some other things which are said about this sort of rule, but I myself have trusted the most plausible account. This scheme of rule is called by the Romans *interrēgnum*.

Nevertheless, tumults arose from the suspicion that the patricians were converting the state to an oligarchy and did not wish for a king. The people revolted from this. When all agreed that a ruler

7.5
Ἡ Ἀρχὴ τοῦ Νόμα Πομπιλίου

Τούτων δὲ περὶ τὸν Ῥωμύλον συμβεβηκότων βασιλεύεσθαι μὲν ἐδόκει πᾶσιν, ἔρις δέ τις καὶ στάσις ἐφύετο τοῖς ἐν Ῥώμῃ οὐχ ὑπὲρ ἀνδρὸς μόνον ἡγεμονεύσοντος, ἀλλὰ καὶ πότερον τῶν γενῶν παρέξει τὸν ἄρξοντα. τοῖς τε γὰρ μετὰ Ῥωμύλου πρώτοις συνοικίσασι τὴν πόλιν οὐκ ἀνεκτὸν ἐδόκει παρ' αὐτῶν προσληφθέντας τοὺς Σαβίνους εἰς πολιτείαν ἄρχειν τῶν δεξαμένων βιάζεσθαι· οἱ Σαβῖνοι δὲ ἑτέρωθεν, ὅτι τοῦ Τατίου θανόντος μόνον εἴασαν τὸν Ῥωμύλον ἄρχειν, ἐξ ἑαυτῶν ἠξίουν αἱρεθῆναι τὸν ἄρξοντα.

Ἦριζον μὲν οὖν οὕτω τὰ μέρη ἑκάτερα, μετεώρου δ' ἐπὶ τούτοις ὄντος τοῦ πολιτεύματος οἱ πατρίκιοι πεντήκοντα καὶ ἑκατὸν ὄντες ἔταξαν ἕκαστον ἐν μέρει τοῖς βασιλικοῖς παρασήμοις κοσμούμενον θύειν τε τοῖς θεοῖς καὶ χρηματίζειν, ἓξ μὲν τῆς νυκτὸς ὥρας, ἓξ δὲ τῆς ἡμέρας. ἡ γὰρ διανομὴ τῶν καιρῶν κατὰ τὸ ἴσον ἑκάστου καὶ πρὸς τοὺς ἄρχοντας καλῶς ἔχειν ἐδόκει καὶ πρὸς τοὺς ἀρχομένους αὐτούς· ἀφήρει γὰρ τὸν φθόνον ἡ ταχίστη τῆς ἐξουσίας ἀπόθεσις, ὁρώντων τῶν ἀρχομένων τῆς αὐτῆς ἡμέρας τε καὶ νυκτὸς τὸν αὐτὸν ἰδιώτην ἐκ βασιλέως γινόμενον. οἶδα μὲν οὖν καὶ ἕτερά τινα περὶ τῆς τοιαύτης εἰρημένα ἀρχῆς, ἀλλ' αὐτὸς τῷ πιθανωτέρῳ ἐθέμην. τὸ δὲ σχῆμα τῆς ἀρχῆς τοῦτο μεσοβασιλεία Ῥωμαίοις ὠνόμαστο.

Ἀλλὰ καὶ οὕτως ἐξ ὑπονοίας ἐφύοντο θόρυβοι, ὑποπτευομένων τῶν πατρικίων εἰς ὀλιγαρχίαν τὴν πολιτείαν περιστᾶν καὶ μὴ βούλεσθαι βασιλεύεσθαι· ἐκ δὲ τούτου κατεστασίαζον. ὁμονοησάντων δὲ πάντων αἱρεθῆναι τὸν

should be selected, the Sabines gave the first choice to the Romans, who selected from among the Sabines a certain Numa Pompilius, a man who was well known by all for his virtue. Ambassadors from Rome were therefore sent to him. Numa did not live in Rome, but stayed among the Sabines and and inhabited the city of the Quirites. His father was a well-renowned man named Pomponius, who was adorned by every virtue which can be bestowed by either nature or education. For this reason, he has a great name and a certain amount of fame, such that Tatius, when he ruled with Romulus, married Numa to his only daughter, Tatia. She remained married to Numa for three years before she departed from this life. Numa then left behind his occupations in the city so that he could live for the most part in the open, where he wished to spend time in the meadows and glades.

Therefore, the ambassadors came from Rome to call him to the throne as he was finishing his fortieth year of life. He declined their offer. The ambassadors, however, pressed hard upon him, having contrived every way to persuade him, and fearing lest the city should again fall into rebellion and civil war, since there was no other man to whom both parts of the state would readily grant their assent. In private, even, Numa's father urged his son to accept the throne as a divine gift and a form of service of god, as well the sort of thing which would be the source of noble and great deeds for a wise man; moreover, it would serve as a pledge of goodwill and friendship between the entire Sabine race and a powerful, thriving city.

Bound by these considerations, Numa sacrificed to the gods and then set out to Rome, where the senate and people sang his praises and greeted him warmly. When they then called together the assembly and presented him with the regal insignia, he ordered them to hold off and said that he needed Jupiter, too, to ratify his rule. He then ascended the Capitoline, made a sacrifice, and then finally taking up the regal insignia, he descended once again.

βασιλεύσοντα, οἱ Σαβῖνοι τοῖς Ῥωμαίοις προτέροις τὴν αἵρεσιν ἔδοσαν·οἱ δ' ἐκ Σαβίνων εἵλοντο Νόμαν Πομπίλιον, ὄντα ἄνδρα γνώριμον πᾶσι δι' ἀρετήν. στέλλονται γοῦν πρὸς ἐκεῖνον ἐκ Ῥώμης πρέσβεις· οὐ γὰρ ἐν τῇ Ῥώμῃ μετῴκιστο, ἀλλ' ἐν Σαβίνοις ἦν καὶ πόλιν ᾤκει τὴν Κυριτῶν, πατρὸς ὢν Πομπωνίου ἀνδρὸς εὐδοκίμου, πᾶσαν ἀρετὴν φύσει τε καὶ παιδείᾳ ἐξησκημένος. ὅθεν καὶ ὄνομα μέγα καὶ δόξαν εἶχεν, ὡς καὶ Τάτιον τὸν τῷ Ῥωμύλῳ συμβασιλεύσαντα κηδεστὴν αὐτὸν ἐπὶ Τατίᾳ θέσθαι τῇ θυγατρί, ἣν μίαν ἐκεῖνος ἐγείνατο· ἣ δέκα ἐπὶ τρισὶν ἐνιαυτοὺς τῷ Νόμᾳ συνοικήσασα μετήλλαξε τὴν ζωήν. ὁ δὲ Νόμας ἐκλιπὼν τὰς ἐν ἄστει διατριβὰς ἀγραυλεῖν τὰ πολλὰ καὶ διατρίβειν ἤθελεν ἐν λειμῶσι καὶ ἄλσεσιν.

Ἧκον οὖν ἀπὸ Ῥώμης οἱ πρέσβεις καλοῦντες ἐπὶ τὴν βασιλείαν αὐτὸν ἤδη τεσσαρακοστὸν ἔτος ἀνύοντα· ὁ δὲ ἀπείπατο. οἱ πρέσβεις δ' ἐνέκειντο, πάντα τρόπον πείσειν αὐτὸν μηχανώμενοι, καὶ δεόμενοι μὴ τὴν πόλιν αὖθις εἰς στάσιν ἐμβαλεῖν καὶ ἐμφύλιον πόλεμον, οὐκ ὄντος ἑτέρου πρὸς ὃν ἄμφω τὰ μέρη συννεύσουσιν. ἰδίᾳ μέντοι καὶ ὁ πατὴρ παρεκίνει τὸν Νόμαν δέξασθαι τὴν ἀρχὴν ὡς θεῖον δῶρον καὶ ὑπηρεσίαν θεοῦ καὶ πράξεων καλῶν καὶ μεγάλων ἀνδρὶ φρονίμῳ τε καὶ χρηστῷ ἐσομένην αἰτίαν, σύνδεσμόν τε τῇ πατρίδι καὶ παντὶ τῷ Σαβίνων ἔθνει εὐνοίας τε καὶ φιλίας πρὸς πόλιν δυνατὴν καὶ ἀκμάζουσαν.

Τούτοις ἐνδεδωκὼς ὁ Νόμας θύσας τοῖς θεοῖς προῆγεν εἰς Ῥώμην· ὑπήντα δὲ ἡ βουλὴ καὶ ὁ δῆμος εὐφημοῦντες καὶ χαίροντες. ἐπεὶ δὲ κατέστησαν εἰς τὴν ἀγοράν, προσφερομένων αὐτῷ τῶν βασιλικῶν παρασήμων, ἐπισχεῖν κελεύσας ἔφη δεῖσθαι καὶ θεοῦ τὴν βασιλείαν ἐμπεδοῦντος αὐτῷ. ἄνεισιν οὖν εἰς τὸ Καπιτώλιον, καὶ θύσας, οὕτω τε τὴν βασιλικὴν ἀναλαβὼν ἐσθῆτα, κατέβαινε.

As soon as he assumed the throne, he disbanded the group of three hundred, which Romulus always had about his person. For he said that it was not right to distrust those who trusted him, nor did he think it a worthy thing to be king of those who distrusted him. Next, he undertook to make the city, which to this point was rough and warlike, a bit more civilized and peaceful. He forbade the erection of an anthropomorphic statue of Zeus by the Romans. For this reason, there was among them no drawn or sculpted images of the god, and in a period of 170 years they made no anthropomorphic images in the shrines which they erected, considering it irreligious to manufacture things which were superior to our hands, and because it was not possible to seize upon a god otherwise than as he intended. Numa also ordered that sacrifices be made bloodless by using barley and libations, because it was necessary that the gods, being as they were guardians of peace and justice, should be pure of any murder. Nor, he insisted, should anyone listen nor watch anything pertaining to the gods as a distraction, nor with little care; rather, they should take a break from other affairs and focus their attention upon piety, since it was the most important matter. From these things and many more which I have not mentioned, Numa fashioned from custom the religious constitution of the state for the people of the time. They say that Numa himself was so hung up on his hopeful notions about the gods that when it was announced to him in the middle of a sacrifice that Rome's enemies were at hand, he simply smiled and said, "Ah, but I am sacrificing." Numa also distributed the land, which Romulus had acquired in war, to the needy citizens; in so going, he alleviated their poverty, which he considered a necessary cause of injustice, and turned it into the pursuit of agriculture, which he thought helped to soften the people while making their love of a powerful peace much more keenly perceptible.

Ἡ Ἀρχὴ τοῦ Νόμα Πομπιλίου

Παραλαβὼν δὲ τὴν ἀρχὴν πρῶτον μὲν τὸ τῶν τριακοσίων διέλυσε σύστημα, οὓς περὶ τὸ σῶμα Ῥωμύλος εἶχεν ἀεί· οὐ γὰρ δεῖν ἀπιστεῖν πιστεύουσιν ἔλεγεν, οὐδὲ βασιλεύειν ἀπιστούντων ἠξίου·εἶτα τὴν πόλιν ἐκ σκληρᾶς καὶ πολεμικῆς ἐπεχείρει μαλακωτέραν ποιῆσαι καὶ εἰρηνικωτέραν. ἀνθρωποειδῆ τε καὶ ζωόμορφον εἰκόνα θεοῦ ἀνιστᾶν Ῥωμαίοις ἀπείρηκεν· ὅθεν οὐδ' ἦν παρ' αὐτοῖς οὔτε γραπτὸν οὔτε πλαστὸν εἶδος θεοῦ, ἐν ἑκατὸν δὲ πρὸς ἑβδομήκοντα ἔτεσι ναῶν αὐτοῖς ἀνεγειρομένων οὐδὲν ἔμμορφον ἐποίουν ἀφίδρυμα, ὡς οὔτε ὅσιον ἀφομοιοῦν τοῖς χείροσι τὰ βελτίονα οὔτε ἐφάπτεσθαι ἄλλως θεοῦ δυνατὸν ἢ νοήσει. καὶ τὰς θυσίας δὲ ἀναιμάκτους ποιεῖσθαι ἐθέσπισε δι' ἀλφίτων τε καὶ σπονδῆς δεῖν γὰρ τοὺς θεούς, εἰρήνης καὶ δικαιοσύνης φύλακας ὄντας, φόνου καθαροὺς εἶναι· μήτε δὲ ἀκούειν τι τῶν θείων μήτε ὁρᾶν ἐν παρέργῳ καὶ ἀμελῶς, ἀλλὰ σχολὴν ἄγοντας ἀπὸ τῶν ἄλλων καὶ προσέχοντας τὴν διάνοιαν ὡς πράξει μεγίστῃ τῇ περὶ τὴν εὐσέβειαν. ἐκ δὲ τούτων καὶ ἄλλων πλειόνων, ἃ διὰ τὸ πλῆθος παρήκαμεν, διάθεσιν πρὸς τὸ θεῖον τοῖς τότε ἀνθρώποις ἐξ ἐθισμοῦ ὁ Νόμας ἐνεποίησεν. αὐτὸν δὲ οὕτω φασὶν εἰς τὸ θεῖον ἀνηρτῆσθαι ταῖς ἐλπίσιν ὥστε προσαγγελίας αὐτῷ θύοντί ποτε γινομένης ὡς ἐπέρχονται πολέμιοι μειδιᾶσαι καὶ εἰπεῖν "ἐγὼ δὲ θύω." καὶ τὴν χώραν δὲ ἣν αἰχμῇ Ῥωμύλος ἐκτήσατο διένειμεν οὗτος τοῖς ἀπόροις τῶν πολιτῶν, ἀφαιρῶν ἐξ αὐτῶν τὴν ἀπορίαν, ὡς ἀνάγκην τῆς ἀδικίας ποιητικήν, καὶ τρέπων εἰς γεωργίαν, ὡς ταύτης ἐξημερούσης τὸν δῆμον καὶ δριμὺν εἰρήνης δυναμένης ἐμποιεῖν ἔρωτα.

It is also said that January and February were added by Numa to the other months, who set out that the year should be reckoned as twelve months in accordance with the course of the moon. The calendar year had among the Romans previously been ten months, just as among some of the barbarians it was three months, and of the Greeks it was four months with the Arcadians, six months with the Acharnians. The calendar year was one month among the Egyptians, and subsequently four months. For that reason, the Egyptians seem wondrously ancient (though they are not), because they bring a preposterous weight of years into their genealogy when they match the number of years to the number of months. Numa also gave January its place at the beginning of the year.

Thus, as Numa accustomed his subjects to justice and piety, he removed all considerations of war. For, not only was the Roman people made tame by Numa's sense of divine order and gentle disposition, but the beginnings of change overtook even the surrounding cities as they were all seized by desire for peace and justice, and a zeal for planting crops, raising children in peace, and reverencing the gods. No war, no uprising, no revolution in the city is recorded during Numa's reign, nor is it recorded that any hatred, any envy, or any conspiracy was contrived against Numa through desire to seize the throne. Numa had a daughter named Pompilia, and he gave her in marriage to Marcius. From Pompilia was born Numa's grandson Ancus Marcius, who reigned after Tullus Hostilius. When Ancus was five, Numa left him behind as he died, having been worn down by old age and a mild illness. He had lived for 83 years and ruled for 43.

Λέγεται δὲ καὶ τὸν Ἰανουάριον καὶ τὸν Φεβρουάριον παρ' αὐτοῦ τοῖς μησὶ προστεθῆναι, δωδεκάμηνον κατὰ τὸν τῆς σελήνης δρόμον νομοθετήσαντος λογίζεσθαι τὸν ἐνιαυτόν, δεκάμηνον πρόσθεν ὄντα, ὡς ἐνίοις τῶν βαρβάρων τρίμηνον, καὶ τῶν Ἑλλήνων Ἀρκάσι μὲν τετράμηνον, τοῖς δὲ Ἀκαρνᾶσιν ἑξάμηνον. Αἰγυπτίοις δὲ μηνιαῖος ἦν ὁ ἐνιαυτός, εἶτα τετράμηνος· διὸ καὶ ἀρχαιότατοι δοκοῦσιν εἶναι, καίτοι μὴ ὄντες, πλῆθος ἀμήχανον ἐτῶν ἐπὶ ταῖς γενεαλογίαις εἰσάγοντες, ἅτε δὴ τοὺς μῆνας εἰς ἐτῶν τιθέμενοι ἀριθμόν. καὶ τὸν Ἰανουάριον δὲ Νόμας εἰς ἀρχὴν τοῦ ἔτους ἀπένειμεν.

Οὕτω δὲ δικαιοσύνῃ καὶ εὐσεβείᾳ συνεθίσαντος τὸ ὑπήκοον, ἐξῄρητο πάντῃ τὰ τοῦ πολέμου. οὐ γὰρ μόνον ὁ Ῥωμαίων δῆμος ἡμέρωτο τῇ τοῦ βασιλέως εὐνομίᾳ καὶ πρᾳότητι, ἀλλὰ καὶ τὰς κύκλῳ πόλεις ἀρχὴ μεταβολῆς ἔλαβε, καὶ πόθος εἰσερρύη πάντας εἰρήνης καὶ τοῦ δικαίου, γῆν φυτεύειν καὶ τέκνα τρέφειν ἐν ἡσυχίᾳ καὶ σέβεσθαι θεούς. οὔτε γὰρ πόλεμος οὔτε στάσις οὔτε νεωτερισμὸς περὶ πολιτείας ἱστόρηται Νόμα βασιλεύοντος, οὐδ' ἐπ' ἐκεῖνον ἔχθρα τις ἢ φθόνος ἢ σύστασις ἀνδρῶν καὶ ἐπιβουλὴ δι' ἔρωτα βασιλείας γενέσθαι ποι ἀναγέγραπται. θυγατέρα δ' ἐσχηκὼς Πομπιλίαν, Μαρκίῳ ταύτην ἐξέδοτο· ἐξ ἧς Μάρκιος Ἄγκος θυγατριδοῦς ἐτέχθη αὐτῷ, ὃς μετὰ Τοῦλλον Ὀστίλλιον ἐβασίλευσε. τοῦτον πενταετῆ καταλιπὼν ὁ Νόμας ἐτελεύτησεν, κατὰ μικρὸν ὑπὸ γήρως καὶ νόσου μαλακῆς ἀπομαραινόμενος, χρόνον τριετῆ τοῖς ὀγδοήκοντα προσβιώσας, βασιλεύσας ἔτη ἐπὶ τρισὶ τεσσαράκοντα.

7.6

The Reign of Tullus Hostilius

Upon the death of Numa, who had left behind no successor, Tullus Hostilius was selected as king by the people and senate. He, holding in contempt most of the ways of Numa, eagerly strove to emulate Romulus, and he therefore got himself up for battles and provoked the people. At one point, when the Albans had undertaken a plundering expedition against the Romans, the people of both cities set out for war against each other. Before it came to blows, they were reconciled, and it seemed suitable to both sides that they should each live together in one city. When each one held to its own and thought it proper that the people of the other side should move to their own, they abandoned this proposal. Thereupon, they came into conflict over the question of political supremacy. As neither side would cede control to the other, they decided to engage in a contest to decide which side would govern. It did not seem right to engage in a full-blown military contest, nor were they inclined to submit the decision to single combat. There were among both the Romans and the Albans sets of triplets, who were born of twin mothers, and were of equal age and strength. The triplets on the Roman side were called the Publii Horatii, and those on the Alban side were the Curiatii. They were then thrown into battle against each other and disregarded any previous ties of kinship which they shared. They armed themselves, and having arrayed themselves in the middle of the field, they called upon their protector deities and looked uninterruptedly at the sun. When they came up against each other, they fought at first as a group, and then one-by-one. Finally, when two of the Romans had fallen and all three of the Albans had been wounded, Horatius – because he could not

7.6

Ἡ Ἀρχὴ τοῦ Ὁστιλλίου Τούλλου

Τοῦ δὲ Νόμα τελευτήσαντος καὶ μηδένα καταλιπόντος διάδοχον, Ὁστίλλιος Τοῦλλος ἡρέθη παρὰ τοῦ δήμου καὶ τῆς βουλῆς. ὃς τὰ πλεῖστα τῶν τοῦ Νόμα χλευάσας ἠθῶν τὸν Ῥωμύλον ἐζήλωσε, καὶ πρὸς μάχας αὐτός τε ὥρμα καὶ τὸν δῆμον ἠρέθιζεν. ἁρπαγῆς γοῦν γενομένης παρὰ Ῥωμαίων ἐξ Ἀλβανῶν, ὥρμησαν πρὸς μάχην ἑκάτεροι· πρὸ δὲ τοῦ συμβαλεῖν κατηλλάγησαν, καὶ ἐς μίαν πόλιν ἀμφοῖν ἐδόκει συνοικῆσαι τοῖς γένεσιν. ἑκάστου δὲ τῆς οἰκείας ἐχομένου καὶ τὸ ἕτερον εἰς ταύτην ἀξιοῦντος μεταναστεῦσαι, ἀπέστησαν τοῦ σκοποῦ. εἶτα περὶ τῆς ἡγεμονίας διηνέχθησαν· ὡς δὲ οὐδεὶς τῷ ἑτέρῳ παρεχώρει αὐτῆς, ἀγωνίσασθαι συνέθεντο περὶ τῆς ἀρχῆς. οὔτε δὲ τοῖς στρατοπέδοις ὅλοις ἐδόκει μαχέσασθαι οὔτε μὴν μονομαχίᾳ κριθήσεσθαι. ἦσαν δὲ παρ' ἀμφοῖν τρίδυμοι ἀδελφοί, ἐκ μητέρων γεγονότες διδύμων, ἰσήλικές τε καὶ ἰσοπαλεῖς τὴν ἰσχύν·ἐκαλοῦντο δὲ οἱ μὲν τῶν Ῥωμαίων Πουπλιοράτιοι, οἱ δὲ τῶν Ἀλβανῶν Κουριάται. τούτους εἰς μάχην προεβάλοντο, παρ' οὐδὲν τὴν πρὸς ἀλλήλους αὐτῶν συγγένειαν θέμενοι. οἱ δὲ ὁπλισάμενοι καὶ ἐν τῷ μεταιχμίῳ τῶν στρατοπέδων ἀντιπαραταξάμενοι θεούς τε ὁμογνίους ἀνεκαλοῦντο καὶ συνεχῶς ἀνέβλεπον πρὸς τὸν ἥλιον. συμβαλόντες δὲ ποτὲ μὲν ἀθρόοι, ποτὲ δὲ καὶ καθ' ἕνα ἐμάχοντο. τέλος δὲ τῶν μὲν Ῥωμαίων τῶν δύο πεσόντων, τῶν δὲ Ἀλβανῶν ἁπάντων τρωθέντων, ὁ Ὁράτιος ὁ κατάλοιπος, ὅτι τοῖς τρισὶν ἅμα, εἰ καὶ

encounter all three Albans even though he himself were unwounded – turned himself to flight so that they would be separated from each other in their pursuit of him. Because they were torn asunder in the chase, Hostilius was able to set upon each one individually and slay them all, for which feat he was honored. He was, however, brought to trial for murder when he killed his sister, who had expressed her grief upon seeing him carrying the spoils of her slain cousins. He pled his case before an assembly of the people, and was released from the charge.

The citizens of Alba Longa then fell under the power of the Romans (though they later disregarded their pledges) and they were summoned as subjects to assist the Romans in battle. When it was learned that they had shifted to the enemies in an opportune part of the battle and had set upon the Romans, they were punished. Many of them were stretched out and torn asunder, including their leader Mettius Fufetius; the rest were compelled to emigrate, and their city of Alba Longa was razed to the ground, after having in some way been considered the mother city to Rome for 500 years.

Tullus Hostilius was famed for his rather violent power against his enemies, but he was careless of religion. When a pestilential illness befell him, though, even he inclined somewhat to fear the gods. He is said to have ended his life after being struck by lightning, or perhaps as the result of a conspiracy formed by Ancus Marcius, the grandson (as has been noted) of Numa. Tullus Hostilius reigned over the Romans for thirty-two years.

ἄτρωτος ἦν, οὐκ ἠδύνατο ἀντιτάξασθαι, ἐνέκλινεν, ὡς ἂν διώκοντες αὐτὸν σκεδασθῶσι κἀπειδὴ πρὸς τὴν δίωξιν διεσπάρησαν, ἑκάστῳ ἐπιτιθέμενος ἅπαντας διεχρήσατο. κἀντεῦθεν τετίμητο· ὅτι δὲ καὶ τὴν ἀδελφὴν προσαπέκτεινεν, ὀλοφυρομένην, ἐπεὶ τὰ τῶν ἀνεψιῶν σκῦλα ἑώρα φέροντα τὸν Ὁράτιον, φόνου ἐκρίθη· ἐς δὲ τὸν δῆμον ἔκκλητον αἰτήσας ἀφείθη.

Οἱ δὲ Ἀλβανοὶ τότε μὲν ὑπήκοοι τῶν Ῥωμαίων ἐγένοντο, ὕστερον δὲ τὰς συνθήκας ἀθετήσαντες, καὶ ὡς ὑπήκοοι πρὸς συμμαχίαν κληθέντες, μεταθέσθαι δὲ πρὸς τοὺς πολεμίους ἐν τῷ καιρῷ τῆς μάχης ἐπιχειρήσαντες καὶ συνεπιθέσθαι Ῥωμαίοις, γνωσθέντες ἐκολάσθησαν· καὶ πολλοὶ μὲν ἐκτάνθησαν καὶ ὁ αὐτῶν ἐξηγούμενος Μέττιος, οἱ ἄλλοι δὲ μετανάστασιν ἔπαθον, καὶ ἡ πόλις αὐτῶν Ἄλβα κατεσκάφη, πεντακόσιά που ἔτη Ῥωμαίοις νομισθεῖσα μητρόπολις.

Πρὸς μὲν οὖν τοὺς πολεμίους ὁ Τοῦλλος κράτιστος ἔδοξε, τοῦ θείου δὲ παρημέλει. νόσου δ' ἐνσκηψάσης λοιμώδους καὶ αὐτὸς νοσήσας εἰς δεισιδαιμονίαν ἀπέκλινεν. ἐσχηκέναι μέντοι τοῦ βίου λέγεται τέλος καταφλεχθεὶς ὑπὸ κεραυνῶν, ἢ ἐπιβουλευθεὶς ὑπὸ Μαρκίου Ἄγκου, ὃς θυγατριδοῦς ἐτύγχανεν, ὡς εἴρηται, τοῦ Νόμα. ἐβασίλευσε δὲ Ῥωμαίων ἔτη δύο ἐπὶ τριάκοντα.

7.7

The Reign of Ancus Marcius

When Tullus Hostilius died, Ancus Marcius succeeded to the throne, which he took with the approval of the Roman people. He was not perfectly formed in regard to his hand, because his arm had been mutilated; it was for this reason that he received the name "Ancus." Though he was a reasonable man, he was compelled to change, and turned himself toward military affairs. For, on account of the destruction of Alba Longa, the other Latin cities feared that they themselves might suffer something similar, and so they held themselves in hostility to the Romans while Tullus Hostilius, whom they feared as a bitter enemy, still lived. Because, however, they thought that Ancus Marcius could easily be attacked with impunity on account of his peaceful mindset, the Latins set upon the land and plundered it. Ancus, reasoning that war could be the cause of peace, set upon those who had set upon the Romans, and he seized their cities, one of which he razed to the ground. He treated many of the citizens of these captured cities as prisoners, and forced some others to emigrate to Rome. As the Roman population increased and their land holdings grew in proportion, those from neighboring areas were vexed and made war against the Romans. Whereupon, the Romans overcame the people of Fidenae in a siege, and distressed the Sabines by falling upon them as they were scattered and taking the field. By instilling fear in the others, they prepared them, however unwilling, to make peace. After all of this, the life of Ancus Marcius came to an end, after he had reigned for twenty four years and given much care to the gods, as had his grandfather Numa.

7.7

Ἡ Ἀρχὴ τοῦ Ἄγκου Μαρκίου

Ἐπεὶ δ' Ὁστίλλιος ἐτελεύτησε, διεδέξατο τὴν βασιλείαν ὁ Μάρκιος, παρ' ἑκόντων τῶν Ῥωμαίων ταύτην λαβών. ἦν δὲ τὴν χεῖρα οὐκ ἄρτιος· τὴν γὰρ ἀγκύλην πεπήρωτο, ὅθεν καὶ Ἄγκος ἐπώνυμον ἔσχηκεν. ἐπιεικὴς δὲ ὢν ἠναγκάσθη μεταβαλέσθαι, καὶ πρὸς στρατείας ἐτράπετο. οἱ γὰρ λοιποὶ Λατῖνοι διά τε τὸν τῆς Ἄλβης ὄλεθρον καὶ περὶ ἑαυτῶν δεδοικότες μή τι πάθωσιν ὅμοιον δι' ὀργῆς μὲν εἶχον Ῥωμαίους, ἕως δὲ περιῆν ὁ Τοῦλλος, δεδιότες ἐκεῖνον ὡς μάχιμον, συνεστέλλοντο. τὸν δὲ Μάρκιον εὐεπίθετον ἡγησάμενοι διὰ τὸ εἰρηναῖον τῆς γνώμης, τῇ τε χώρᾳ ἐπῆλθον καὶ αὐτὴν ἐλήισαντο. συνεὶς δ' ἐκεῖνος εἰρήνης εἶναι τὸν πόλεμον αἴτιον, ἐπιτίθεται τοῖς ἐπιθεμένοις καὶ ἀντημύνατο, καὶ πόλεις εἷλεν αὐτῶν, ὧν μίαν κατέσκαψεν, καὶ πολλοῖς τῶν ἁλόντων ὡς αἰχμαλώτοις ἐχρήσατο, καὶ ἐς τὴν Ῥώμην δὲ συχνοὺς ἑτέρους μετῴκισεν. αὐξανομένων δὲ τῶν Ῥωμαίων καὶ τῆς χώρας σφίσι προστιθεμένης οἱ πλησιόχωροι ἤχθοντο καὶ ἑαυτοὺς Ῥωμαίοις ἐξεπολέμωσαν· ὅθεν αὐτῶν Φιδηνάτας μὲν πολιορκίᾳ ἐκράτησαν, Σαβίνους δ' ἐκάκωσαν, αὐτοῖς τε προσπεσόντες ἐσκεδασμένοις καὶ τὸ σφῶν ἑλόντες στρατόπεδον, ἑτέρους δ' ἐκφοβήσαντες εἰρηνεῖν καὶ ἄκοντας παρεσκεύασαν. καὶ ἐπὶ τούτοις Μαρκίῳ ἐπέλιπε τὸ βιώσιμον, εἴκοσιν ἐνιαυτοὺς καὶ τέσσαρας ἄρξαντι, καὶ πολλὴν τοῦ θείου κατὰ τὸν πάππον Νόμαν ποιουμένῳ τὴν ἐπιμέλειαν.

The Reign of Lucius Tarquin

Lucius Tarquinius then claimed the throne for himself. He was the son of Demaratus of Corinth, who had fled to the Tyrsenian city of Tarquinia, where he married a native woman; together, they had a son named Lucumo. He received many things from his father, including the fact that he would, on account of being a foreigner, he would never mix with the chief men of Tarquinia, and on this account he removed himself to Rome. Once he arrived there, he decided to change his name while he was changing his city, and so he took the name Lucius Tarquinius, from the city in which he had formerly lived. It is said that as he was wandering to the city, an eagle flew down and removed the hat which he wore upon his head; after it ascended into the air and made a great noise, it again descended and replaced the hat on his head; after this occurrence, Lucius Tarquinius entertained no small hopes and set about establishing himself in Rome with considerable zeal and energy. Consequently, it was only a short time before he came to associate with the chief men of the state. He was liberal and profuse with his money, and he won over the powerful men in the city with his wit and keen understanding. He was therefore elevated to patrician status and given a place in the senate by Ancus Marcius, and was made a general; moreover, Ancus entrusted the care of his own children and the throne to Tarquinius. Lucius Tarquinius showed himself to be a good man by giving money to the poor who needed it, and always being ready to help a fellow citizen if necessary. He never did or said a trifling thing to anyone. If he ever received a good turn from another, he extolled the deed, but if he were ever done ill by another, he either made no mention of the harm, or made it sound like a minor thing unworthy of notice; and not only did he

7.8

Ἡ Ἀρχὴ τοῦ Λουκίου Ταρκυνίου

Λούκιος δὲ Ταρκύνιος τὴν ἀρχὴν ᾠκειώσατο, ὃς Δημαράτου μὲν ἦν παῖς Κορινθίου, φυγόντος δὲ καὶ εἰς πόλιν Τυρσηνίδα Ταρκυνίαν ἐγκατοικήσαντος ἐξ αὐθιγενοῦς γυναικὸς ἐκείνῳ ἐτέχθη, Λουκούμων ὀνομασθείς. πολλὰ μέντοι πατρόθεν διαδεξάμενος, ὅτι μὴ τῶν πρωτείων παρὰ τῶν Ταρκυνησίων ὡς ἔπηλυς κατηξίωτο, πρὸς τὴν Ῥώμην μεταναστεύει, τῇ πόλει καὶ τὴν κλῆσιν συμμεταθέμενος, καὶ μετωνομάσθη Λούκιος Ταρκύνιος ἐκ τῆς πόλεως, ἐν ᾗ παρῴκει. λέγεται δὲ μετοικιζομένου ἀετὸς καταπτὰς ἁρπάσαι τὸν πῖλον ὃν εἶχεν ἐπὶ τῆς κεφαλῆς, καὶ μετεωρισθεὶς καὶ κλάγξας ἐπὶ πολὺ αὖθις αὐτὸν ἐφαρμόσαι τῇ αὐτοῦ κεφαλῇ, ὡς ἐντεῦθεν μηδὲν ἐλπίσαι μικρὸν καὶ προθύμως τῇ Ῥώμῃ ἐγκατοικῆσαι·ὅθεν τοῖς πρώτοις οὐ μετὰ πολὺ συνηρίθμητο. τῷ τε γὰρ πλούτῳ χρώμενος ἀφειδέστερον, συνέσει τε καὶ εὐτραπελίᾳ τοὺς δυνατοὺς οἰκειούμενος, ἐς τοὺς εὐπατρίδας καὶ τὴν βουλὴν κατελέχθη παρὰ Μαρκίου, καὶ στρατηγὸς ἀπεδείχθη, καὶ τὴν τῶν παίδων ἐκείνου ἐπιτροπείαν καὶ τῆς βασιλείας πεπίστευτο. ἐδείκνυε γὰρ ἑαυτὸν ἀγαθὸν ἄνδρα, χρημάτων τε τοῖς δεομένοις μεταδιδοὺς καὶ ἑαυτὸν ἕτοιμον παρέχων εἴ τις δέοιτο αὐτοῦ εἰς βοήθειαν· φαῦλον δέ τι οὔτ' ἔπραττεν οὔτ' ἔλεγεν οὐδενί. καὶ εἴ τι πρός τινων εὖ ἔπασχεν, ἐξῆρε τὸ γινόμενον, εἰ δέ τι καὶ ἐπαχθέστερον αὐτῷ γένοιτο, ἢ οὐδ' ἐλογίζετο τὸ λυποῦν ἢ καὶ φαυλίσας παρελογίζετο, οὐ μόνον τε οὐκ ἠμύνετο τὸν λελυπηκότα, ἀλλὰ καὶ εὐηργέτει. τούτοις αὐτόν τε τὸν Μάρκιον καὶ τοὺς περὶ αὐτὸν ἐχειρώσατο, καὶ δόξαν ἀνδρὸς ἐκτήσατο σοφοῦ τε καὶ ἀγαθοῦ.

abstain from chastizing the one who had injured him, but he even did him a favor in turn. In this way, he won over Marcius and the men around him, and earned the reputation of a wise and good man.

This opinion, however, did not last. When Ancus Marcius died, Lucius Tarquinius did wrong by Marcius' sons, and made the throne his own. When the senate and people were on the verge of selecting the sons of Marcius as their rulers, Tarquinius went to hold an interview with the most powerful of the senators, and sent the two orphan boys off to a hunt; and by what he did and said he contrived to have the throne voted to himself. Having thus made himself the master of Roman political affairs, he managed the Romans in such a way as to prevent the two boys from ever being chosen as kings. As he made the sons of Ancus more accustomed to luxury he charmed their souls and bodies into destruction. He lived in fear because he operated this way, and so he girded himself about with force in assembly meetings. He enlisted into the senate and patrician order about two-hundred men who were favorably disposed toward him. In this way, he placed the senate and many of the common people under his own influence. He also transformed his clothing into something more befitting his greatness. This took the form of a toga and a tunic which were entirely purple, inlaid with gold, as well as a crown set with gold stones and an ivory chair. After all of this, other people holding the imperial throne enjoyed absolute political supremacy. He also paraded in triumphs on a four-horse chariot, and had twelve lictors through his life.

Indeed, Tarquinius Priscus would have accomplished many other startling reforms, if a certain Attus Naevius (who was a finer augur than any who had ever lived) had not prevented him from altering the arrangement of the tribes. Tarquinius was enraged by his opposition, and sought to entirely discredit Attus' craft. He therefore put a razor and a whetstone in his cloak, and went among the people

Ἀλλ' οὐ προσέμεινε μέχρι τέλους αὐτῷ ἡ ὑπόληψις. τοῦ Μαρκίου γὰρ τελευτήσαντος κακῶς περὶ τοὺς ἐκείνου διετέθη δύο υἱεῖς, καὶ τὴν βασιλείαν ἐσφετερίσατο. τῆς τε γὰρ βουλῆς καὶ τοῦ δήμου τοὺς τοῦ Μαρκίου παῖδας χειροτονεῖν μελλόντων, ἐκεῖνος τῶν βουλευτῶν τε τοὺς δυνατωτάτους μετῆλθε, καὶ τοὺς ὀρφανοὺς πόρρω ποι πέμψας εἰς θήραν, οἷς τε εἶπε καὶ οἷς ἔπραξεν αὐτῷ τὴν βασιλείαν ψηφίσασθαι παρεσκεύασεν, ὡς ἀνδρωθεῖσιν αὐτὴν δῆθεν τοῖς παισὶν ἀποδώσοντι. ἐγκρατὴς δὲ καταστὰς τῶν πραγμάτων οὕτω τοὺς Ῥωμαίους διέθετο ὥστε μηδέποτε ἐθελήσειν ἀνθελέσθαι τοὺς παῖδας ἐκείνου· καὶ τὰ μειράκια δὲ πρὸς ῥᾳστώνην ἐθίζων τάς τε ψυχὰς αὐτῶν καὶ τὰ σώματα σὺν χάριτι δή τινι ἔφθειρε. δεδιὼς δὲ καὶ οὕτως ἔχων, ἰσχὺν ἑαυτῷ ἐν τῷ συνεδρίῳ περιεποιήσατο. τοὺς γὰρ φιλίως αὐτῷ ἐκ τοῦ δήμου διακειμένους περὶ διακοσίους ἐς τοὺς εὐπατρίδας ἐνέγραψε καὶ τοὺς βουλευτάς, καὶ οὕτω τήν τε γερουσίαν ὑφ' ἑαυτὸν καὶ τοὺς πολλοὺς ἐποιήσατο. καὶ τὴν στολὴν πρὸς τὸ μεγαλοπρεπέστερον ἤμειψεν· ἡ δὲ ἦν ἱμάτιον καὶ χιτὼν ὁλοπόρφυρα καὶ χρυσόπαστα, στέφανός τε λίθων χρυσοδέτων καὶ σκῆπτρον δίφρος τε ἐλεφάντινα, οἷς καὶ μετὰ ταῦτα οἵ τε ἄλλοι καὶ οἱ τὴν αὐτοκράτορα ἔχοντες ἡγεμονίαν ἐχρήσαντο. καὶ τεθρίππῳ ἐν τοῖς ἐπινικίοις ἐπόμπευσε, καὶ ῥαβδούχους διὰ βίου δώδεκα ἔσχε.

Πάντως δὲ καὶ ἄλλα πλείω ἐκαινοτόμησεν ἄν, εἰ μή τις Ἄττος Ναούιος τὰς φυλὰς αὐτὸν βουληθέντα μετακοσμῆσαι κεκώλυκεν, ὃς οἰωνιστὴς ἦν οἷος οὐχ ἕτερος γέγονε. τοῦτον ὑβρίσαι, διὰ τὴν ἐναντίωσιν ὀργισθείς, καὶ τὴν τέχνην ἐξουθενῆσαι διεμελέτησεν ὁ Ταρκύνιος. λαβὼν οὖν ἐν τῷ κόλπῳ ἀκόνην τε καὶ ξυρὸν ἐς τὸν δῆμον παρῆλθεν, ἔχων ἐν νῷ τμηθῆναι τῷ ξυρῷ τὴν ἀκόνην, πρᾶγμα τῶν ἀδυνάτων·εἰπών τε

with the intention of cutting the whetstone with the razor – a clearly impossible task. When he began to lay out his plans and Attus began to speak out against him most violently, he did not cave in but rather said, 'If you are not speaking against me simply from your love of argument, but are indeed telling the truth, tell me whether what I now have in mind will occur.' Attus, divining immediately what was meant, said, 'Indeed, my king – what you wish will come to pass.' Tarquinius then responded, 'Then take that whetstone, and cut it with that blade. This is what I had in mind.' Attus then took the whetstone immediately and cut it asunder. Tarquinius was amazed, and offered to Attus various honors, including the honor of a bronze statue; he also ceased to reform civic institutions, but began to employ Attus as his advisor in all things.

Later, Tarquinius waged war against the Latin tribes who were rebelling, and subsequently he fought against the Sabines who were aided by the Etruscans; he conquered them all. When he learned that a certain one of the Vestal Virgins (who were ordered to preserve their maidenhood throughout their lives) had engaged in indiscreet intercourse with a man, he had an oblong passage dug underground, in which he placed a couch and a table with an abundance of food. He had the ruined woman sent down there, and after she was led into the chamber, he had it sealed off. Thus, from that event, the custom prevailed that those priestesses who did not take care of their chastity were punished. The men who so defiled these women were forced to place their heads upon cloven logs in the forum, and after being stripped naked and degraded, were deprived of their lives.

The sons of Marcius then set upon Tarquinius, since he did not pass the throne on to them, but instead preferred a certain Tullius who was born to him by a captive woman. This indeed was a thing which had caused the nobles substantial distress. The sons of Marcius therefore enlisted the help of some of these nobles and plotted against

ὅσα ἐβούλετο, ἐπεὶ Ἄττος ἀντέλεγεν ἐντονώτατα, μηδὲν ὑφιέμενος "εἰ μὴ φιλονείκως ἀντιλέγεις" ἔφη "ἀλλ' ἀληθῆ λέγεις, ἐπὶ πάντων τούτων ἀπόκριναί μοι εἰ ὃ κατὰ νοῦν ἔχω ποιῆσαι γενήσεται." ὁ δὲ Ἄττος αὐτοῦ που οἰωνισάμενος παραυτίκα "καὶ πάνυ γε" εἶπεν "ὦ βασιλεῦ, ὃ διανοῇ ἔσται ἐπιτελές." "οὐκοῦν" ἔφη "τὴν ἀκόνην ταύτην λαβὼν τῷ ξυρῷ τούτῳ διάτεμε· τοῦτο γὰρ γενέσθαι διανενόημαι." ὁ δὲ ἔλαβέ τε αὐτὴν εὐθὺς καὶ διέκοψε. θαυμάσας δὲ ὁ Ταρκύνιος ἄλλας τε τιμὰς ἐκείνῳ παρέσχε καὶ χαλκῆς εἰκόνος ἠξίωσε, καὶ οὐδὲν ἔτι τῆς πολιτείας ἠλλοίωσε, πρὸς πάντα τε συμβούλῳ τῷ Ἄττῳ ἐκέχρητο.

Μαχεσάμενος δὲ Λατίνοις ἀποστατήσασιν, ἔπειτα καὶ Σαβίνοις εἰς τὴν Ῥωμαΐδα ἐμβαλοῦσι συμμαχουμένοις ὑπὸ Τυρσηνῶν, ἁπάντων ἐκράτησε. τῶν δὲ τῆς Ἑστίας ἱερειῶν, ἃς παρθενεύειν διὰ βίου νενόμισται, φωράσας τινὰ συμφθαρεῖσαν ἀνδρί, ὑπόγεών τινα κατασκευάσας ὑποδρομὴν προμήκη, κλίνην τε θεὶς ἐν αὐτῇ καὶ λύχνον καὶ τράπεζαν σιτίων ὑπόπλεων, ἐκεῖ τὴν φθαρεῖσαν προπεμπομένην ἐκόμισε, καὶ ζῶσαν εἰσαγαγὼν ἐγκατῳκοδόμησε. καὶ οὕτω τὰς τὴν παρθενίαν μὴ τηρησάσας τῶν ἱερειῶν ἐξ ἐκείνου τιμωρεῖσθαι κεκράτηκεν· οἱ δὲ ταύτας αἰσχύνοντες εἰς ξύλον τὸν αὐχένα δίκρουν ἐμβάλλονται ἐν τῇ ἀγορᾷ, καὶ μετὰ τοῦτο γυμνοὶ αἰκιζόμενοι ἀποψύχουσιν.

Ἐπέθεντο μέντοι τῷ Ταρκυνίῳ οἱ τοῦ Μαρκίου παῖδες, ἐπεὶ μὴ τῆς ἀρχῆς αὐτοῖς παρεχώρει, ἀλλά τινα Τούλλιον τεχθέντα οἱ ἐξ αἰχμαλωτίδος προῆγε πάντων ὃ δὴ μάλιστα τοὺς εὐπατρίδας ἐλύπει. ὧν τινας προσεταιρισάμενοι αὐτῷ ἐπεβούλευσαν, δύο τινὰς χωριτικῶς ἐσταλμένους, ἀξίναις καὶ δρεπάνοις ὡπλισμένους, αὐτῷ ἐπιθέσθαι παρασκευάσαντες. οἳ

Tarquinius; their plan was to send, in rustic fashion, two men armed with axes and sickles to attack Tarquinius. When it happened that they did not encounter Tarquinius in public, they went to the doors of his regal home, indeed striving against each other as they needed to come into his presence. When they met him, they fell into an argument with each other, and while Tarquinius paid attention to one of the men as he was pleading his case, the other man slew him.

ἐπεὶ μὴ ἀγοράζοντι τῷ Ταρκυνίῳ ἐνέτυχον, ἐπὶ τὰς θύρας τῶν βασιλείων ἧκον, ἀλλήλοις δῆθεν διαμαχόμενοι, καὶ οἱ ἐλθεῖν εἰς ὄψιν ἐδέοντο. καὶ τυχόντες τούτου εἰς λόγους ἀλλήλοις ἀντικατέστησαν, καὶ δικαιολογουμένῳ τῷ ἑνὶ προσέχοντα τὸν Ταρκύνιον ὁ ἕτερος κατειργάσατο.

7.9

The Reign of Servius Tullius

Tarquinius Priscus met such an end after reigning for thirty-eight years. Thereupon, Tullius became the king of the Romans with the assistance of Tarquinius' wife, Tanaquil. His mother, a woman named Ocrisia, was the bedmate of a man named Servius Tullius. She was taken in war and brought to Tarquinius. She gave birth, either already being pregnant when still in her home city, or conceiving after its capture – both stories are told. Tullius, as he was nearing the end of childhood, fell asleep upon a seat during the day, and fire seemed to project forth from his head. When Tarquinius saw this, he took the boy up with eagerness, and when he had reached the proper age, enlisted him among the patricians and the senate.

The murderers of Tarquinius were caught, while his wife and Tullius – once they learned of the plot – did not make his death known to all. They took his body away and made a pretense of tending to it as though he were still alive, and they added further assurance to others that Tullius, taking up the throne, would abdicate it when her own sons came to manhood. When the people arrived, they clamored, and Tanaquil, emerging from the upper chambers, told them 'Do not fear. My husband is alive, and you will soon see him. But, so that he may take some rest to recover himself, and lest his lack of strength stand in the way of public affairs, he has entrusted the management of the state to Tullius for the present moment.' Thus she spoke; the people accepted Tullius not unwillingly, for he seemed to be a good man.

When Tullius then took up the management of public affairs, he followed, for the most part, the injunctions of Tarquinius. When

7.9

Ἡ Ἀρχὴ τοῦ Σερουίου Τουλλίου

Ὁ μὲν οὖν Ταρκύνιος τοιοῦτον ἔσχε τέλος, τριάκοντα καὶ ὀκτὼ βασιλεύσας ἐνιαυτούς, τὴν δὲ τῆς Ῥώμης βασιλείαν ὁ Τούλλιος διεδέξατο, συνεργίᾳ τῆς τοῦ Ταρκυνίου γυναικὸς Τανακυιλίδος. τοῦτον δὲ γυνή τις Ὀκρισία καλουμένη, Σερουίου Τουλλίου ἀνδρὸς Λατίνου εὐνέτειρα ἐν τῷ πολέμῳ ἁλοῦσα καὶ τῷ Ταρκυνίῳ ἐξαιρεθεῖσα, τέτοκεν, ἢ ἐγκύμων οἴκοθεν οὖσα ἢ συλλαβοῦσα μετὰ τὴν ἅλωσιν· λέγεται γὰρ ἀμφότερα. οὗτος ἐς παῖδας ἤδη τελῶν ἐπὶ δίφρου μεθ' ἡμέραν κατέδαρθε, καὶ πῦρ ἀπὸ τῆς αὐτοῦ κεφαλῆς πολὺ ἐδόκει ἐξάλλεσθαι. ὅπερ ἰδὼν ὁ Ταρκύνιος διὰ σπουδῆς ἦγε τὸν παῖδα, καὶ εἰς ἡλικίαν ἀφιγμένον τοῖς εὐπατρίδαις καὶ τῇ γερουσίᾳ συνέταξε.

Συλληφθέντων οὖν τῶν τοῦ Ταρκυνίου φονέων, μαθοῦσα ἡ ἐκείνου γυνὴ καὶ ὁ Τούλλιος τὴν παρασκευὴν τῆς ἐπιβουλῆς οὐ φανερὸν αὐτίκα τὸν τοῦ Ταρκυνίου θάνατον ἔθεντο, ἀλλ' ἀνελόμενοι αὐτὸν ὡς ἔτι ἐμπνέοντα ἐθεράπευον δῆθεν, κἀν τούτῳ πίστεις ἀλλήλοις ἔδοσαν ὥστε τὸν Τούλλιον τὴν ἀρχὴν εἰληφότα τοῖς παισὶν αὐτῆς ἀνδρωθεῖσιν ἐκστῆναι ταύτης. ἐπεὶ δὲ τὸ πλῆθος συνδραμὸν ἐθορύβει, προκύψασα ἐκ τῶν ὑπερῴων ἡ Τανακυιλὶς "μὴ φοβεῖσθε" ἔφη·"ὁ γὰρ ἀνήρ μου καὶ ζῇ καὶ ὑμῖν μετ' ὀλίγου ὀφθήσεται. ἵνα δὲ αὐτός τε σχολάζων ὑγιασθῇ καὶ μή τι τοῖς πράγμασιν ἐκ τῆς αὐτοῦ ἀσθενείας εἴη ἐμπόδιον, Τουλλίῳ κατά γε τὸ παρὸν τὴν τῶν κοινῶν ἐπιτρέπει διοίκησιν." εἶπεν ἐκείνη ταῦτα·οἱ δὲ τὸν Τούλλιον οὐκ ἀκουσίως ἐδέξαντο ἀγαθὸς γὰρ ἀνὴρ ἐδόκει.

Ἐγχειρισθεὶς οὖν ἐκεῖνος τὴν τῶν κοινῶν οἰκονομίαν, τὰ πλείω κατ' ἐντολὰς δῆθεν διῴκει τοῦ Ταρκυνίου. ὡς δ' ἐν πᾶσιν

he saw among the multitude the men who had murdered Tarquinius, he employed a strategem to lead them to the senate house: he pretended that Tarquinius was still alive. Some of them were condemned and executed, but the sons of Marcus had fled to the Volsci in fear. Tullius then revealed the death of Tarquinius and openly took up the kingship. First, he exiled the sons of Tarquinius so as to entrust the sole rule to himself, and he then subsequently turned his attention to public service; with the aim of easily winning over the rabble rather than the nobles, he gave them property and land, while also preparing to free the slaves and enroll them in the tribes. When the powerful men of the state felt grieved by this, he ordered that those who were being freed should perform some service in turn for those who freed them. The nobles then spread the report that he held the kingship without receiving it from anyone, but had mustered the people together through demagoguery. Having said so many enticing things to them, he caused the entire state to be voted over to him. Tullius, however, responded that he had other ambitions, and enlisted some of them in the senate. The ancient plebeians had less power than the patricians, but as time went on (and except in the case of an interregnum or religious occasion) they had an equal share with the patricians, and differed from them in no way but their shoes. For, the patricians wore shoes with a fashionable interweaving of the straps and stylish inscription, so that they could easily be noticed as descending from the original hundred men who sat in the senate. They say that the inscription was the Greek letter Rho, either as the clear mark of the number 100, or as the first letter of the Roman name.

Tullius thus won the plebeians over to his side, yet fearing the chance of a rebellion, he entrusted the greatest and strongest parts of the commonwealth to the most powerful. They worked in mutual concord, and managed public affairs as well as possible. They waged a few wars against the Veiians and the Etruscans more generally, but

ἑώρα πειθαρχοῦντας αὐτῷ, τοὺς αὐτόχειρας τοῦ Ταρκυνίου πρὸς τὴν γερουσίαν παρήγαγε, διὰ τὴν ἐπιβουλὴν τάχα ἔτι γὰρ ζῆν ἐκεῖνον προσεποιεῖτο. καὶ οἱ μὲν καταψηφισθέντες ἀπέθανον, οἱ δὲ τοῦ Μαρκίου υἱοὶ φοβηθέντες εἰς Οὐολούσκους κατέφυγον. κἀκεῖνος τότε τόν τε θάνατον τοῦ Ταρκυνίου ἐξέφηνε καὶ φανερῶς τῆς βασιλείας ἐπείληπτο. καὶ πρῶτον μὲν τοὺς τοῦ Ταρκυνίου παῖδας προυβάλλετο ὡς αὐτὸς τὴν ἡγεμονίαν ἐπιτροπεύων, εἶτα πρὸς θεραπείαν τοῦ δήμου ἐτράπετο, ὡς ῥᾷστα μᾶλλον τὸν ὅμιλον ἢ τοὺς εὐπατρίδας ὑποποιησόμενος, χρήματά τε αὐτοῖς ἐδίδου καὶ γῆν ἑκάστῳ προσένειμε καὶ τοὺς δούλους ἐλευθεροῦσθαι καὶ φυλετεύεσθαι παρεσκεύασεν. ἀχθομένων δ' ἐπὶ τούτοις τῶν δυνατῶν, ἔταξέ τινα τοὺς ἐλευθερωθέντας τοῖς ἐλευθερώσασι σφᾶς ἀνθυπουργεῖν. ὡς δὲ χαλεπῶς εἶχον οἱ εὐπατρίδαι αὐτῷ, καὶ διεθρόουν ἄλλα τε καὶ ὅτι μηδενὸς αὐτὸν ἑλομένου τὴν ἀρχὴν ἔχει, συναγαγὼν τὸν δῆμον ἐδημηγόρησε· καὶ πολλὰ ἐπαγωγὰ διαλεχθεὶς αὐτῷ οὕτω διέθετο ὡς αὐτίκα πᾶσαν αὐτῷ τὴν βασιλείαν ἐπιψηφίσασθαι. ὁ δὲ αὐτοὺς ἀμειβόμενος ἄλλα τε ἐφιλοτιμήσατο καὶ ἐς τὸ συνέδριόν τινας αὐτῶν ἐνέγραψεν οἳ πάλαι μὲν ἐν πλείστοις ἧττον ἔφερον τῶν εὐπατριδῶν, τοῦ χρόνου δὲ προϊόντος, πλὴν τῆς μεσοβασιλείας καὶ τῶν ἱερωσυνῶν, τῶν ἴσων μετεῖχον τοῖς εὐπατρίδαις, καὶ διέφερον ἄνευ τῶν ὑποδημάτων οὐδέν. τοῖς γὰρ εὐπατρίδαις τὰ ὑποδήματα ἀστικὰ τῇ τε ἐπαλλαγῇ τῶν ἱμάντων καὶ τῷ τύπῳ τοῦ γράμματος ἐκεκόσμητο, ἵν' ἐκ τούτων δοκοῖεν ἀπὸ τῶν ἑκατὸν ἀνδρῶν τῶν κατ' ἀρχὰς βουλευσάντων κατιέναι. τὸ γράμμα δὲ ῥῶ φασιν εἶναι, ἢ τοῦ ἀριθμοῦ τῶν ἑκατὸν ἐκείνων ἀνδρῶν δηλωτικὸν ὂν ἢ ὡς τοῦ τῶν Ῥωμαίων κατάρχον ὀνόματος.

Τὸν μὲν οὖν ὅμιλον οὕτως ὁ Τούλλιος ᾠκειώσατο, δείσας δὲ μή τις στάσις συμβῇ, τὰ πλεῖστα καὶ ἰσχυρότατα τῶν κοινῶν

this involved nothing worth writing down. Tullius also wanted even more to reconcile the rest of the Latins to the Romans, so he persuaded them to construct a shrine at the public expense in Rome, which they dedicated to Artemis. Yet, disagreement arose as to who should tend the shrine. A Sabine man led a rather beautiful cow to the altar, as if to sacrifice it to Artemis because of a certain oracle. The oracle stated that the one who sacrificed the cow would increase the greatness of his country. When one of the Romans heard this, he came to the man, and told him that it was first necessary to purify the cow in the river. Thus he persuaded the Sabine man, and taking the cow as if to guard it, he sacrificed it himself. When the Sabine man revealed the oracle, the Latins yielded the erection of the shrine to the Romans, and in other respects honored the Romans as their superiors.

Thus all of those things stood. Tullius then married his daughters to the sons of Tarquinius Priscus, and after promising to hand the throne over to them, he put it off with one excuse after another. They did not take the matter lightly, but felt offended; yet Tullius considered them of little concern, and continued to push the Romans toward freedom and democracy, which the Tarquins found even more galling. The younger Tarquin, though he resented all of this, nevertheless bore it. It did not, however, appear just in the older Tarquin's estimation to tolerate Tullius. Since he found that his wife (who was Tullius' daughter) did not agree with him, he killed her himself, while arranging for the other Tullia to kill his brother with poison. Once he had fallen in with his brother's wife, they both contrived together against the life of Tullius. Since many of the senators and patricians were ill-disposed toward Tullius, Tarquinius persuaded them to take up against him, and he went with them immediately to the senate house with his wife in tow. He said many things to remind those who were present of his father's great deeds, and leveled many criticisms against Tullius. When Tullius heard of all

τοῖς δυνατωτέροις ἐπέτρεψε· καὶ οὕτω σφίσιν αὐτοῖς συνεφρόνησαν καὶ τὸ δημόσιον διήγαγον ἄριστα. καὶ πολέμους δέ τινας πρός τε τοὺς Οὐιέντας καὶ πρὸς ἅπαντας τοὺς Τυρσηνοὺς ἐπολέμησεν, ἐν οἷς οὐδὲν ἐπράχθη συγγράμματος ἄξιον. τοὺς Λατίνους δ' ἐπὶ μᾶλλον Ῥωμαίοις βουληθεὶς οἰκειώσασθαι, νεών τινα ἐκ χρημάτων κοινῶν ἐν τῇ Ῥώμῃ κατασκευάσαι πέπεικε. καὶ τοῦτον ἀνέθεσαν τῇ Ἀρτέμιδι. περὶ δὲ τῆς νεωκορίας αὐτοῦ διεφέροντο. κἂν τούτῳ Σαβῖνος ἀνὴρ βοῦν ἦγε περικαλλῆ πρὸς τὴν Ῥώμην, ὡς ἔκ τινος χρησμοῦ θύσων αὐτὴν τῇ Ἀρτέμιδι. ὁ δὲ χρησμὸς τὸν ἐκείνην θύσαντα ἔλεγε τὴν πατρίδα ἐπαυξήσειν. τοῦτο δέ τις τῶν Ῥωμαίων μαθὼν προσῆλθεν αὐτῷ καὶ πρότερον εἶπε δεῖν ἐν τῷ ποταμῷ ἁγνισθῆναι, καὶ εἰπὼν ἔπεισε, καὶ πείσας ἔλαβε τὴν βοῦν ὡς φυλάξων, καὶ λαβὼν ἔθυσεν. ἐκφήναντος δὲ τοῦ Σαβίνου τὸ λόγιον οἱ Λατῖνοι καὶ τῆς τοῦ ἱεροῦ προστασίας τοῖς Ῥωμαίοις ἐξέστησαν καὶ ἐς τἄλλα ὡς κρείττονας σφῶν ἐτίμων αὐτούς.

Καὶ ταῦτα μὲν οὕτως· ὁ Τούλλιος δὲ τοῖς Ταρκυνίοις τὰς θυγατέρας συνῴκισε, καὶ τὴν βασιλείαν αὐτοῖς ἀποδώσειν ἐπαγγειλάμενος ἄλλοτε ἄλλο τι προφασιζόμενος ἀνεβάλλετο. οἱ δὲ οὐδὲν ὑγιὲς ἐφρόνουν, ἀλλὰ ἤχθοντο. ὁ δ' ἐν οὐδενὶ λόγῳ τούτους πεποίητο, καὶ τοὺς Ῥωμαίους πρὸς τὸ δημοκρατικὸν ἐνῆγε καὶ τὸ ἐλεύθερον. ἔτι δὲ μᾶλλον ἐπὶ τούτοις ἤσχαλλον οἱ Ταρκύνιοι. ἀλλ' ὁ μὲν νεώτερος, κἂν ἐχαλέπαινεν, ἔφερεν, τῷ δὲ τῷ χρόνῳ προήκοντι οὐκέτι τοῦ Τουλλίου ἐδόκει ἀνέχεσθαι. ἐπεὶ δὲ μὴ συνευδοκοῦσαν εὕρισκε τὴν γυναῖκα καὶ τὸν ὁμαίμονα, αὐτὸς μὲν τὴν γυναῖκα, τὸν δ' ἀδελφὸν διὰ τῆς γυναικὸς ἐκείνου φαρμάκοις διέφθειρε, καὶ συναφθεὶς τῇ συνεύνῳ τοῦ ἀδελφοῦ τῷ Τουλλίῳ σὺν αὐτῇ ἐπεβούλευε. καὶ πολλοὺς τῶν τε βουλευτῶν καὶ τῶν εὐπατριδῶν αἰτίας ἔχοντας κατὰ τοῦ Τουλλίου πείσας συνάρασθαί οἱ, ἐξαπιναίως μετ' αὐτῶν εἰς τὸ συνέδριον

this, and said a word after standing up for himself in haste, Tarquinius grabbed him, picked him up, and threw him down the stairs of the senate house. Tullius, terrified by the boldness of Tarquinius and the fact that he had no assistance, neither said nor did anything further. Tarquinius, immediately seizing the throne, sent some men to intercept Tullius on his way and kill him. Tullius' daughter, after expressing her love in the senate house and proclaiming him king, went off toward the palace and drove her chariot over the body of her father where it lay.

παραγέγονεν, ἑπομένης αὐτῷ καὶ τῆς γυναικὸς Τουλλίας· καὶ πολλὰ μὲν εἶπε τῆς τοῦ πατρὸς ἀξίας τοὺς παρόντας ἀναμιμνήσκων, πολλὰ δ' ἀπέσκωψε πρὸς τὸν Τούλλιον. ἐπεὶ δ' ἐκεῖνος ταῦτα μαθὼν ἐπέστη σπουδῇ, καί τι δὴ καὶ ἐφθέγξατο, συνήρπασεν αὐτὸν καὶ ἐξάρας ὦσε κατὰ τῶν πρὸ τοῦ βουλευτηρίου ἀναβαθμῶν. καὶ ὁ μέν, ταραχθεὶς πρὸς τὴν τοῦ Ταρκυνίου τόλμαν καὶ ὅτι οὐδέ τις αὐτῷ ἐπεκούρησεν, οὔτ' εἶπεν ἔτι οὐδὲν οὔτ' ἐποίησε· Ταρκύνιος δὲ τήν τε βασιλείαν εὐθὺς παρὰ τῆς βουλῆς ἔλαβε καὶ πέμψας τινὰς τὸν Τούλλιον κομιζόμενον οἴκαδε διεχρήσατο. ἡ δὲ θυγάτηρ ἐκείνου ἐν τῷ βουλευτηρίῳ τὸν ἄνδρα καταφιλήσασα καὶ βασιλέα προσαγορεύσασα καὶ ἀπιοῦσα πρὸς τὰ βασίλεια τὸ ὄχημα κατὰ τοῦ νεκροῦ τοῦ πατρὸς ὡς εἶχεν ἐπήλασεν.

7.10

The Reign of Tarquin the Proud

Thus Tullius ruled and thus Tullius died, after a reign of forty four years. When Tarquinius seized the throne, he set an armed guard around himself after the example of Romulus, which he made use of both at night and through the day, whether he were at home or in public. For, after what he and his wife had done to his father-in-law, they were afraid of everyone else. He made preparations as a tyrant would, and he took up and got rid of the most powerful men both in and out of the senate. He killed those whom he had a case against in the open, and killed the others in secret. He banished some others. He did not destroy only those who were favorable to Tullius, but also all of those who were unfavorably disposed toward the monarchy, and he thus reduced the strongest part of the senate and the equestrian order. He knew that he was hated by all of the plebeians. On that account, he did not replace any of the men who were killed, but undertook to dissolve the senate altogether, and did not enlist anyone in it or communicate anything worthy of note to those who were in it. He was in the habit of calling them together, not so that they could conduct any necessary business, but so that their thinned ranks could be clear to all, and he thereupon treated them with contempt. He performed most business either by himself or with the aid of his sons. He was not easy to approach or address, and he treated everyone with contempt and savagery; both he and his sons began to behave more tyrannically toward everyone. For that reason, and also because he had his suspicions of his bodyguards, he enlisted an armed band from the Latin tribes and mixed them with his Roman contingent, so that the Latins, in receiving an equal share from him, would turn the

7.10

Ἡ Ἀρχὴ τοῦ Ταρκυνίου τοῦ Σουπέρβου

Οὕτω μὲν οὖν ὁ Τούλλιος ἦρξε καὶ οὕτως ἀπέθανε βασιλεύσας τέσσαρας ἐνιαυτοὺς ἐπὶ τεσσαράκοντα, ὁ Ταρκύνιος δὲ τὴν βασιλείαν παρειληφὼς δορυφόρους κατὰ Ῥωμύλον ἑαυτῷ περιέστησεν, καὶ νύκτωρ καὶ μεθ' ἡμέραν αὐτοῖς καὶ οἰκουρῶν καὶ ἀγοράζων ἐκέχρητο. ἐξ ὧν γὰρ αὐτὸς εἰς τὸν κηδεστὴν καὶ ἡ γυνὴ πρὸς τὸν πατέρα ἐποίησαν, καὶ τοὺς λοιποὺς ἐδεδίεσαν. ἐπεὶ δὲ ὡς τυραννήσων παρεσκευάσατο, τοὺς δυνατωτάτους τῶν βουλευτῶν καὶ τῶν ἄλλων συλλαμβάνων ἐκτίννυεν, οἷς μὲν αἰτίαν εἶχεν ἐπενεγκεῖν φανερῶς ἀναιρῶν, οὓς δὲ λάθρα·ἐνίους δέ γε καὶ ὑπερώριζεν. οὐ γὰρ τοὺς τῷ Τουλλίῳ προσκειμένους μόνους, ἀλλὰ καὶ τοὺς πρὸς τὴν μοναρχίαν συναραμένους αὐτῷ προσαπώλλυε, καὶ οὕτω τὸ κράτιστον τῆς βουλῆς καὶ τῆς ἱππάδος ἀνάλωσε. μισεῖσθαί τε ὑπὸ παντὸς τοῦ δήμου ἐπίστευε·διὸ οὐ δὲ ἀντικαθίστη τὸ παράπαν ἀντὶ τῶν ἀπολλυμένων τινάς, ἀλλὰ καὶ τὴν γερουσίαν καταλῦσαι παντελῶς ἐπιχειρήσας οὔτε ἀντεισῆγεν ἐς αὐτὴν οὐδένα οὔτε τοῖς οὖσιν ἐπεκοίνου τι λόγου ἄξιον. συνεκάλει μὲν γὰρ αὐτούς, οὐ μὴν ὥστε τι τῶν ἀναγκαίων συνδιοικεῖν, ἀλλ' ἵνα δήλη αὐτῶν ἡ βραχύτης γίνοιτο ἅπασι, κἀντεῦθεν καταφρονοῖντο· τὰ δὲ πλεῖστα καθ' ἑαυτὸν ἢ καὶ μετὰ τῶν υἱέων ἔπραττε. δυσπρόσιτός τε καὶ δυσπροσήγορος ἦν, καὶ τῇ ὑπεροψίᾳ καὶ τῇ ὠμότητι ὁμοίως ἐχρῆτο πρὸς ἅπαντας, καὶ τυραννικώτερον αὐτός τε καὶ οἱ παῖδες αὐτοῦ προσεφέροντο ἅπασι. διὰ ταῦτα δὲ καὶ τοὺς δορυφόρους ὑπόπτους ἔχων, ἐκ τῶν Λατίνων προσηταιρίσατο δορυφορικόν, καὶ ἐς τὰς τῶν Ῥωμαίων τάξεις Λατίνους ἐνέμιξεν, ἵνα οἱ μὲν Λατῖνοι ἰσομοιρίας τοῖς Ῥωμαίοις τυχόντες

common sentiment in his favor; he also hoped that the Romans would instill him with less fear when they were no longer left to their own devices, but were forced to arm themselves with the Latins.

Tarquin declared war on Gabii, and because the battle was going badly, he subdued them with a trick. He bid his son to defect to Gabii. In order to put the most convincing spin on this defection, Sextus railed against his father as a tyrant and an oath breaker, and Tarquinius whipped his son and defended himself. Then, according to the agreement, he made his false defection to Gabii, taking along with him some money and companions. The people of Gabii, believing this charade because of Tarquinius' well-known savagery, and because at that time Sextus' reproaches against his father were all true, it seemed that they really were in a feud. They therefore embraced him most heartily, and they then began to make with him many raids on Roman land, which they attacked rather savagely. Then, because he offered money to some men personally, and pressed the attack on their common enemy so mercilessly, he was made general by the people of Gabii and entrusted with the management of their political affairs. After all of this, he sent a man to his father to let him know how things had proceeded, and to ask about what he desired to be done next. Tarquinius said nothing in response to the man, but – that he might not betray what he willed or did not – he led the man to a garden filled with poppy plants. He cut the tallest heads of these off with his staff, and laying them upon the ground, he sent the messenger away. The messenger then reported what had happened to Sextus in total ignorance of what had really transpired. But Sextus understood the meaning of the suggestion, and proceeded to kill off the most prominent citizens of Gabii – some in secret by poison, others with armed assailants, and still others he murdered through the law courts, by fabricating a charge that they intended to ally themselves with his father.

εὔνοιαν αὐτῷ ἐντεῦθεν ὀφείλωσι, καὶ οἱ Ῥωμαῖοι ἧττον ἐκφοβῶσιν αὐτόν, μηκέτι κατὰ σφᾶς ὄντες, ἀλλὰ τοῖς Λατίνοις συνοπλιτεύοντες.

Γαουίνοις δὲ μάχην συνῆψε, καὶ κακῶς μὲν ἠγωνίσατο, δόλῳ δὲ αὐτοὺς ἐχειρώσατο. αὐτομολῆσαι γὰρ αὐτοῖς Σέξτῳ ὑπέθετο τῷ υἱῷ· ἵνα δ' εὐπρόσωπος αὐτῷ τῆς αὐτομολίας πρόφασις γένηται, ἐκεῖνος μὲν τὸν πατέρα φανερῶς ὡς τύραννον καὶ παράσπονδον ἐλοιδόρησεν, ὁ δὲ τὸν υἱὸν ἐμαστίγωσέ τε καὶ ἀντημύνατο. εἶτα κατὰ συνθήκας πρὸς Γαουίνους ἐψευδαυτομόλησε, χρήματά τε καὶ ἑταίρους παρειληφώς. οἱ δέ, πιστεύσαντες τῇ σκηνῇ διά τε τὴν τοῦ Ταρκυνίου ὠμότητα καὶ ὅτι καὶ τότε πολλὰ καὶ ἀληθῆ τὸν πατέρα ἐκακηγόρει κἀντεῦθεν ἐκπεπολεμῶσθαι αὐτῷ ἐδόκει, ἐδέξαντό τε αὐτὸν ἀσμενέστατα καὶ τινας ἐπελεύσεις κατὰ τῆς Ῥωμαϊκῆς χώρας σὺν αὐτῷ ἐποιήσαντο καὶ οὐ μετρίως αὐτῇ ἐλυμήναντο. διὰ ταῦτα γοῦν, καὶ ὅτι χρήματα ἰδίᾳ τέ τισι παρεῖχε καὶ ἐς τὸ κοινὸν ἀνήλισκε δαψιλῶς, ᾑρέθη παρ' αὐτῶν στρατηγὸς καὶ τὴν τῶν πολιτικῶν ἐν αὐτοῖς πραγμάτων ἐπετράπη διοίκησιν. ἐπὶ τούτοις λάθρα πέμψας τινὰ τὰ συμβάντα τε ἐγνώρισε τῷ πατρὶ καὶ πρὸς τὸ μέλλον γνώμην ᾔτησεν ἐξ αὐτοῦ. ὁ δὲ εἶπε μὲν τῷ πεμφθέντι οὐδέν, ἵνα μὴ ἴσως γνωσθεὶς ἑκών τι ἢ ἄκων ἐξείποι, εἰς δὲ κῆπον εἰσαγαγὼν αὐτόν, ἐν ᾧ μήκωνες ἦσαν, τὰς κωδύας αὐτῶν τὰς ὑπερεχούσας ῥάβδῳ κατέκλασε καὶ εἰς γῆν κατεστόρεσε, καὶ οὕτω τὸν ἀγγελιαφόρον ἀπέπεμψε. καὶ ὁ μὲν τὸ πραχθὲν τῷ Σέξτῳ ἀπήγγειλεν, ἀσυνέτως ἔχων τῆς πράξεως, ὁ δὲ τὸν νοῦν συνῆκε τῆς ὑποθέσεως, καὶ τοὺς ἀξιολογωτέρους τῶν Γαουίνων τοὺς μὲν λάθρα φαρμάκοις διέφθειρε, τοὺς δὲ διά τινων δῆθεν λῃστῶν, ἄλλους δὲ καὶ ἐκ δικαστηρίων ἀπέκτεινε, συκοφαντίας κατ' αὐτῶν πρὸς τὸν πατέρα προδοσίας πλαττόμενος.

Herodotus relates a story similar to this. He says that Periander, the son of Cypselus and tyrant of Corinth, sent to Thrasybulus, the tyrant of Miletus, to find out how he could maintain his reign in security. Thrasybulus said nothing in response to the messenger, but took him out to a field where he cut off the tops of corn stalks and tossed them aside; he then sent the messenger back. When he returned and was asked about Thrasybulus' counsel, the messenger said that he had been sent off to a madman; he explained what Thrasybulus had done, and how he had not said anything in response to what he was asked. But Periander understood the meaning of the Thrasybulus' response and killed all of the chief men among the Corinthians.

And then Sextus thus fell upon the people of Gabii; he killed the nobles and gave their possessions to the poor. Subsequently, when some had been killed and the rest were either deceived or entrusted all things to him, he took the city with some of his Roman guards and Gabian deserters (which he had gathered together for that purpose) and gave it to his father. Superbus entrusted the management of the city to his son, while he himself proceeded to conduct various wars against other peoples.

Ὅμοιον δέ τι τούτῳ καὶ ὁ Ἡρόδοτος ἱστορεῖ. Περίανδρον γὰρ τὸν Κυψέλου τύραννον Κορίνθου γενόμενόν φησι πρὸς Θρασύβουλον τὸν Μιλήτου τύραννον διαπέμψασθαι πυνθανόμενον ὅπως αὐτῷ τὰ τῆς ἀρχῆς ἀσφαλῶς ἕξει. τὸν δὲ Θρασύβουλον τῷ ἀπαγγείλαντι ταῦτα μηδὲν ἀποκρίνασθαι, ἀπαγαγόντα δ' εἰς λήιον τῶν ἀσταχύων τοὺς ὑπερέχοντας ἐκτέμνειν τε καὶ ῥιπτεῖν, καὶ οὕτως ἀποπέμψαι τὸν ἐσταλμένον. τὸν δὲ ἐπανελθόντα καὶ τὴν Θρασυβούλου συμβουλὴν ἐρωτώμενον εἰπεῖν εἰς παραπλῆγα πεμφθῆναι, καὶ διηγεῖσθαι ὅσα ἐκεῖνος ἐποίησε, μή τι πρὸς ὃ ἠρωτήθη φθεγξάμενος·τὸν δὲ Περίανδρον συνεικέναι τὸν τοῦ Θρασυβούλου λογισμόν, καὶ τοὺς ὑπερέχοντας τῶν Κορινθίων ἅπαντας ἀπολέσαι.

Καὶ ὁ Σέξτος οὖν οὕτω τοὺς Γαουίνους μετῆλθε, καὶ τοὺς μὲν κρείττους ἀπώλλυε, τῷ πλήθει δὲ τὰ σφῶν διένειμε χρήματα. καὶ μετὰ τοῦτο τῶν μὲν διαφθαρέντων ἤδη, τῶν δὲ λοιπῶν ἠπατημένων καὶ πάντα πιστευόντων αὐτῷ, μετὰ τῶν αἰχμαλώτων Ῥωμαίων καὶ τῶν αὐτομόλων, οὓς πολλοὺς διὰ τοῦτο συνήθροισε, κατέσχε τὴν πόλιν καὶ τῷ πατρὶ παραδέδωκε. καὶ ὃς ἐκείνης τῷ υἱῷ παρεχώρησεν, αὐτὸς δὲ πρὸς ἄλλα ἐπολέμησεν ἔθνη.

7.11

The Fall of Tarquin the Proud

Tarquinius Superbus handed the prophecies of the Sibyl down to the Romans unwillingly. For a certain prophetess, whom the Romans called the Sibyl, came to Rome bearing either three or nine books, which she gave Tarquinius the chance to purchase as she determined the honor of the books. When he paid no heed to her, she burnt either one or three of the volumes. When Tarquinius again dishonored her, she burnt the same portion of the remaining books. As she was about to burn the rest, the augurs compelled Tarquinius to purchase the remaining books, which he purchased for the same price which he would have paid for the full number. He then entrusted them to the guardianship of two senators. Because they did not entirely understand what was written, they sent to Greece and paid two men there to study and interpret the texts. The nearby inhabitants, wishing to know what was explained in the books, bought off Marcus Acillius and transcribed some of the text. Once the crime of Marcus was detected, he was put into a leather sack and thrown into the sea. Subsequently, this was the prevalent punishment used against patricides, so that neither the land, nor the water, nor the sun would be polluted by their deaths.

He constructed a temple on the Tarpeian Hill according to the wish of his father. As the foundation was laid down, the earth split apart and the head of a recently deceased man appeared still full of blood. The Romans therefore sent to an Etruscan soothsayer to inquire about the meaning of the portent. The soothsayer, with the aim of turning this to the advantage of the Etruscans, drew out a diagram upon the earth, in which he drew the situation of Rome and

7.11

Ἡ Ἔκπτῶσις τοῦ Ταρκυνίου τοῦ Σουπέρβου

Τοὺς δὲ τῆς Σιβύλλης χρησμοὺς Ῥωμαίοις καὶ ἄκων προσεποιήσατο. γυνὴ γάρ τις θεόμαντις, ἣν Σίβυλλαν ὠνόμαζον, ἐς τὴν Ῥώμην ἐλήλυθε βιβλία τρία ἢ ἐννέα φέρουσα, καὶ ταῦτα πρίασθαι τῷ Ταρκυνίῳ ἐδίδου καὶ τὴν τιμὴν τῶν βιβλίων ὡρίσατο. ἐκείνου δὲ μὴ προσεσχηκότος αὐτῇ, τὸ ἓν ἢ τὰ τρία τῶν βιβλίων κατέκαυσεν. ὡς δ' αὖθις ὠλιγώρει αὐτῆς ὁ Ταρκύνιος, κἀκ τῶν λοιπῶν ὁμοίως διέφθειρε. μελλούσης δὲ καὶ τὰ ἔτι λοιπὰ καταφλέξειν, ἠνάγκασαν αὐτὸν οἱ οἰωνισταὶ τὰ γοῦν σωζόμενα πρίασθαι. καὶ ὠνήσατο ταῦτα ὅσου τὰ πάντα κτήσασθαι ἔμελλε, καὶ δύο βουλευταῖς ἀνδράσι φυλάσσειν παρέδωκεν. ὡς δ' οὐ πάνυ τῶν γεγραμμένων συνίεσαν, εἰς τὴν Ἑλλάδα στείλαντες δύο ἄνδρας ἐκεῖθεν μισθοῦ ἤγαγον τοὺς ἀναγνωσομένους ταῦτα καὶ ἑρμηνεύσοντας. οἱ δὲ περίοικοι μαθεῖν ἐθελήσαντες ὅ τι ποτὲ τὸ διὰ τῶν βιβλίων εἴη δηλούμενον, τὸν ἕτερον τῶν φυλασσόντων αὐτὰ Μάρκον Ἀκίλλιον χρήμασιν ἀναπείσαντες μετεγράψαντό τινα. γνωσθέντος δὲ τοῦ ἔργου ὁ Μάρκος βύρσαις δύο συρραφείσαις ἐμβληθεὶς κατεποντώθη, ὃ ἐξ ἐκείνου μετέπειτα κατὰ τῶν πατροκτόνων ἐπεκράτησε γίνεσθαι, ἵνα μήτε ἡ γῆ μήτε τὸ ὕδωρ μήτε ὁ ἥλιος μιανθῇ αὐτοῦ θνήσκοντος.

Τὸν δὲ νεὼν τὸν ἐν τῷ Ταρπηίῳ ὄρει κατὰ τὴν τοῦ πατρὸς εὐχὴν ᾠκοδόμει. τῆς δὲ γῆς εἰς τὴν τῶν θεμελίων καταβολὴν ἀναρρηγνυμένης, ἀνδρὸς νεοθνῆτος κεφαλὴ ἀνεφάνη ἔναιμος ἔτι. ἔπεμψαν οὖν Ῥωμαῖοι πρὸς ἄνδρα Τυρσηνὸν τερατοσκόπον ἐρωτῶντες τὸ διὰ τοῦ φανέντος δηλούμενον. ὁ δὲ τὸ σημεῖον εἰς τὴν Τυρσηνίδα μεταθεῖναι μηχανησάμενος, διάγραμμα ἐπὶ τῆς

the Tarpeian Hill. He planned to ask the ambassadors, "Is that Rome? Is that the Hill? Was the head found there?" so that the ambassadors, suspecting nothing, would agree to these statements and the power of the portent would be transferred to the ground on which it was drawn. Thus the soothsayer had planned it, but the ambassadors learned the plan from his son, and so when they were asked these questions, responded "Rome is not there, but in Latium, and the Tarpeian Hill is in the city of the Romans, and the head was found on that hill." Thus, the soothsayer's trick having been avoided, they learned the truth about the portent and announced to their fellow citizens that the Romans would be the strongest and would rule over many. From this, great hope sprung up in their hearts. Thereupon the rock's name was changed to the Capitoline, for in the Roman language *capita* signifies 'head.'

Finding himself short of funds on account of the construction of the aforementioned shrine, Tarquinius waged war against Ardea. From this war, he not only failed to get hold of any money, but also lost his throne; indeed, there had even been certain portents clearly indicating his coming deposition. In his garden, vultures had snatched away some newborn eagles, and in the banquet hall, where he was entertaining some friends, a huge snake appeared and fell upon him and his dinner guests. On this account, he sent his sons Titus and Arruns to Delphi. There, Apollo prophesied that he would fall from the throne when a dog had a human voice, and so Tarquinius was buoyed up by good hopes, thinking that such a thing could never come to pass.

There was also a Lucius Junius, the son of Tarquinius' sister, whose father and brother Tarquinius had murdered. Lucius, fearing for his own safety, pretended to be a fool as a guarantee of his safety, and was thus called 'Brutus' (stupid). The custom among the Latins is to use these kinds of epithets for the nobles. While playing the fool, he

γῆς ἐποιήσατο, καὶ εἰς αὐτὸ τήν τε τῆς Ῥώμης θέσιν ἐντείνας καὶ τὸ Ταρπήιον ὄρος, ἔμελλε τοὺς πρέσβεις ἀνερέσθαι "ἡ Ῥώμη αὕτη ἐστί; τὸ ὄρος τοῦτό ἐστιν; ἡ κεφαλὴ ἐνταῦθα εὑρέθη;" ἵν' ἐκείνων μηδὲν ὑποτοπησάντων καὶ συμφησάντων ἡ δύναμις τοῦ σημείου εἰς τὸ χωρίον ἐν ᾧ διεγέγραπτο μεταστῆι. καὶ ὁ μὲν ταῦτα ἐτεχνάσατο, οἱ δὲ πρέσβεις παρὰ τοῦ υἱέος ἐκείνου μαθόντες τὸ τέχνασμα, ἐρωτώμενοι "οὐκ ἐνταῦθα" εἶπον "οἰκεῖται ἡ Ῥώμη, ἀλλ' ἐν τῷ Λατίῳ, καὶ τὸ ὄρος ἐν τῇ Ῥωμαίων ἐστί, καὶ ἡ κεφαλὴ ἐν τῷ ὄρει ἐκείνῳ εὑρέθη." οὕτω δὲ τῷ τερατοσκόπῳ διακρουσθέντος τοῦ μηχανήματος πᾶσαν ἐκεῖνοι τὴν ἀλήθειαν ἔμαθον καὶ τοῖς πολίταις ἀνήγγειλαν ὅτι κράτιστοι ἔσονται καὶ πλείστων ἄρξουσιν. ἐλπὶς οὖν κἀκ τούτου αὐτοῖς προσεγένετο. κἀντεῦθεν τὸ ὄρος μετωνομάσθη παρ' αὐτῶν Καπιτώλιον· καπίτα γὰρ τῇ Ῥωμαίων διαλέκτῳ ἡ κεφαλὴ ὀνομάζεται.

Δεηθεὶς δὲ χρημάτων εἰς τὴν οἰκοδομὴν τοῦ ναοῦ ὁ Ταρκύνιος Ἀρδεάταις ἐπήνεγκε πόλεμον·ὅθεν οὔτε χρήματα προσεκτήσατο καὶ τῆς βασιλείας ἐξέπεσε. γεγόνασι δ' αὐτῷ καὶ σημεῖά τινα δηλωτικὰ τῆς ἐκπτώσεως. ἔκ τε γὰρ τοῦ κήπου αὐτοῦ γῦπες νεοσσοὺς ἐξήλασαν ἀετῶν, καὶ ἐξ ἀνδρῶνος, ἐν ᾧ συνειστιᾶτο φίλοις, ὄφις μέγας ἐπιφανεὶς αὐτόν τε καὶ τοὺς συσσίτους ἐξέβαλε. διά τοι ταῦτα ἐς Δελφοὺς Τίτον τε καὶ Ἀρροῦντα τοὺς υἱοὺς ἔπεμψε. τοῦ δὲ Ἀπόλλωνος χρήσαντος τότε τῆς ἀρχῆς ἐκπεσεῖσθαι αὐτὸν ὅτε κύων φωνῇ ἀνθρωπίνῃ χρήσαιτο, ἀγαθαῖς ἐλπίσιν ἠώρητο, μὴ οἰηθείς ποτε γενέσθαι τὸ μάντευμα.

Ἦν δὲ Λούκιος Ἰούνιος ἀδελφῆς τοῦ Ταρκυνίου υἱός, οὗ τὸν πατέρα καὶ τὸν ἀδελφὸν ὁ Ταρκύνιος ἔκτεινεν. οὗτος οὖν καὶ περὶ ἑαυτῷ δεδοικὼς μωρίαν προσεποιήσατο, ταύτην ἑαυτοῦ προστησάμενος σώτειραν· διὸ καὶ Βροῦτος ἐπεκλήθη· τοὺς γὰρ

was taken along as a pet by the Tarquin brothers for this journey. Yet, when there, he said that he would erect a statue to the god. This was a stick which appeared to have no use, and this earned him no small degree of mockery; but this stick was like an image of his own dissemblance, for he had hollowed it out and filled it with gold, signifying that he had kept his sharp mind safe and respectable by disguising it with the apparent disgrace of stupidity. When the sons of Tarquinius asked which of the two would inherit their father's throne, the god responded that the one who first kissed his mother would hold power. Brutus, understanding this oracle, fell as though by accident and kissed the ground, rightly judging that this was the mother of all.

This Brutus put down the Tarquins, alleging as his cause both the rape of Lucretia, and that otherwise the Tarquins were hated because of their tyranny and violence. Lucretia was the daughter of Lucretius Spurius, a man of the senate, and she had married Collatinus Tarquinius; she was famed for both her beauty and her wise modesty. Sextus, the son of Tarquinius Superbus, formed a desire to violate her, being not so much desirous of her beauty as he was eager for her chaste reputation. Waiting for Collatinus to be away from the house, he came to her at night and dismissed her guards as though she were his wife. First he attempted to sleep with her by using words, and then he employed violence. When he failed to achieve his purpose, he threatened to cut her down. When it was clear that she cared naught for death, he threatened to lay a slave beside her and kill them both; he would then tell the tale that he had found them sleeping together and slain them. This threat terrified Lucretia, and she feared that she might be believed to have done such a thing, so she consented. After being violated, she placed a dagger under her pillow, and sent for both her husband

εὐήθεις οὕτω τοῖς Λατίνοις ἔθος καλεῖν. πλαττόμενος οὖν τὸν μωραίνοντα, τοῖς τοῦ Ταρκυνίου παισὶν εἰς Δελφοὺς ἀπιοῦσι συμπαρελήφθη ὡς ἄθυρμα. ὁ δὲ καὶ ἀνάθημα φέρειν ἔλεγε τῷ θεῷ· τὸ δ' ἦν βάκτρον τι μηδὲν ἐκ τοῦ φαινομένου ἔχον χρηστόν, ὅθεν καὶ ἐπὶ τούτῳ ὠφλίσκανε γέλωτα. τὸ δ' ἦν οἷον εἰκών τις τῆς κατ' αὐτὸν προσποιήσεως· κοιλάνας γὰρ αὐτὸ λάθρα χρυσίον ἐνέχεεν, ἐνδεικνύμενος δι' αὐτοῦ ὡς καὶ τὸ φρόνημα αὐτῷ τῷ τῆς μωρίας ἀτίμῳ σῴῳ σῶον καὶ ἔντιμον κατακρύπτεται. ἐρομένων δὲ τῶν Ταρκυνίου υἱῶν τίς τὴν βασιλείαν τοῦ πατρὸς διαδέξεται, ἔχρησεν ὁ θεὸς τὸν πρῶτον τὴν μητέρα φιλήσαντα τὸ κράτος ἕξειν. καὶ συνεὶς ὁ Βροῦτος ὡς τυχαίως καταπεσὼν τὴν γῆν κατεφίλησεν, αὐτὴν μητέρα πάντων ὑπάρχειν κρίνας ὀρθῶς.

Οὗτος ὁ Βροῦτος τοὺς Ταρκυνίους κατέλυσεν, αἰτίαν τὸ περὶ τὴν Λουκρητίαν συμβεβηκὸς προστησάμενος, καὶ ἄλλως μισουμένους παρὰ πάντων διὰ τὸ τυραννικόν τε καὶ βίαιον. ἡ δὲ Λουκρητία θυγάτηρ μὲν ἦν Λουκρητίου Σπουρίου, ἀνδρὸς τῶν τῆς συγκλήτου ἑνός, γαμετὴ δὲ Κολλατίνου Ταρκυνίου τῶν ἐπιφανῶν, ἐπί τε κάλλει καὶ σωφροσύνῃ τυγχάνουσα περιβόητος. ταύτην Σέξτος ὁ τοῦ Ταρκυνίου υἱὸς αἰσχῦναι σπούδασμα ἔθετο, οὐχ οὕτω τοῦ κάλλους αὐτῆς ἐρασθεὶς ὅσον τῇ ἐπὶ τῷ σώφρονι δόξῃ ἐπιβουλεύων αὐτῆς. τηρήσας οὖν τὸν Κολλατῖνον τῆς οἰκίας ἀποδημοῦντα, νυκτὸς ἐλθὼν πρὸς αὐτὴν ὡς πρὸς γαμετὴν συγγενοῦς κατέλυσε παρ' αὐτῇ. καὶ πρῶτον μὲν λόγοις ἐπείρα συγγενέσθαι αὐτῇ, εἶτα καὶ βίαν προσῆγεν· ὡς δ' οὐδὲν ἐπέραινεν, ἀποσφάξειν ἠπείλησεν· ὡς δὲ καὶ τοῦ θανάτου κατωλιγώρει, δοῦλον παρακατακλινεῖν αὐτῇ ἐπηπείλησε καὶ ἄμφω κτανεῖν καὶ λόγον διαδώσειν ὡς εὑρὼν αὐτοὺς συγκαθεύδοντας ἔκτεινε. τοῦτο τὴν Λουκρητίαν ἐτάραξε, καὶ φοβηθεῖσα μὴ πιστευθείη ταῦθ' οὕτω γενέσθαι, ἐνέδωκε. καὶ μοιχευθεῖσα ξιφίδιον ὑπὸ τὸ προσκεφάλαιον ἔθετο, καὶ μεταπεμψαμένη τόν τε ἄνδρα καὶ τὸν

and father; Brutus and Publius Valerius followed them. Through tears and wailing, she related the whole affair. Then she added, "I will now do what is proper for me; if you are men, you will avenge me, free yourselves from servitude, and show those tyrants what a sort of wife, and what sort of men they abused." As she said all this, she immediately drew out the dagger and killed herself.

As they heard and saw these things, they grieved exceedingly. Brutus employed Publius as his companion and as one who was eager for the deed; they showed Lucretia's body laid out to many of the people, and announcing what had happened to the rest they roused a hatred against the tyrants. They planned to accept Tarquinius no longer. Having done all of these things and entrusted the management of the city to others, Brutus set out on horse to the army, and he persuaded the soldiers to choose the same course of action as the people had. Tarquinius, when he learned about what had happened and rushed in haste back to the city, was driven away and went to Tarquinii with his children and other followers, with the exception of Tullia who, as the story goes, killed herself.

πατέρα, συνεπομένων αὐτοῖς τοῦ τε Βρούτου καὶ Ποπλίου Οὐαλερίου, κατεδάκρυσε καὶ στενάξασα τὸ δρᾶμα πᾶν διηγήσατο· εἶτα ἐπήγαγε "καὶ ἐγὼ μὲν τὰ πρέποντα ἐμαυτῇ ποιήσω, ὑμεῖς δὲ εἴπερ ἄνδρες ἐστέ, τιμωρήσατε μὲν ἐμοί, ἐλευθερώθητε δὲ αὐτοί, καὶ δείξατε τοῖς τυράννοις οἵων ὑμῶν ὄντων οἵαν γυναῖκα ὕβρισαν." τοιαῦτα εἰποῦσα εὐθὺς τὸ ξιφίδιον ὑφελκύσασα κατέκτεινεν ἑαυτήν.

Ἀκούσαντες δ' ἐκεῖνοι ταῦτα καὶ θεασάμενοι ὑπερήλγησαν. καὶ τῷ Ποπλίῳ συμβούλῳ καὶ προθύμῳ πρὸς τοὔργον ὁ Βροῦτος χρησάμενος τήν τε γυναῖκα πολλοῖς τῶν τοῦ δήμου κειμένην ὑπέδειξε, καὶ πρὸς τοὺς λοιποὺς δημηγορήσας τὸ πρὸς τοὺς τυράννους μῖσος ἐκφῆναι πεποίηκε· καὶ μηκέτι δέξασθαι συνέθεντο τὸν Ταρκύνιον. ταῦτα δὲ πράξας, καὶ τὴν πόλιν ἐπιτρέψας τοῖς ἄλλοις, αὐτὸς πρὸς τὸ στρατόπεδον ἐξιππάσατο, καὶ τὰ αὐτὰ τῷ δήμῳ συνέπεισε καὶ τοὺς στρατιώτας ψηφίσασθαι. ὁ δέ γε Ταρκύνιος τὰ συμβεβηκότα μαθὼν καὶ πρὸς τὴν πόλιν ἐπειχθεὶς ἀπεώσθη, καὶ πρὸς τοὺς Ταρκυνησίους μετὰ τῶν παίδων καὶ τῶν ἄλλων ὁμοφρόνων κατέφυγε, μόνης τῆς Τουλλίας, ὡς λόγος, ἑαυτὴν ἀνελούσης.

7.12

The Republic

Tarquinius Superbus, then, lost his throne after tyrannizing over the people for twenty years. The Romans then bent their favor toward Brutus and selected him as their leader. Lest his leadership should look like regal monarchy, they elected Collatinus Tarquinius, the husband of Lucretia, as his co-ruler, because he was known to hate the tyrants due to the rape of his wife. Some ambassadors from Tarquinius came to Rome to discuss terms of his return. They accomplished nothing, but some other ambassadors came from Tarquinius saying that he was willing to abandon his regal title and desist from the war if the Romans would pay to him, his family, and his attendants a sum which would allow them to live comfortably through life in exile. The resolution of many people was swayed by this, including that of Brutus' colleague Collatinus. Therefore, Brutus ran from the senate house into the forum, and denounced Collatinus as a traitor who delighted in war and the profits of tyranny.

The ambassadors who had been sent to Rome on the pretense of asking for money remained in the city for a while and managed to corrupt some of the nobles, among whom were the sons of Brutus, whom they persuaded to engage in treason. Therefore, as they persuaded them, it seemed right to undertake an oath, and after all of this they returned home. The house was deserted and dark. A certain slave named Vindicius escaped their notice within the house, not by contrivance but by chance. As he lay hidden, he was a witness to their deeds and plans, which involved the murder of the consuls and the surrender of the city; they had related these intentions to Tarquinius through the ambassadors. Once the conspirators had left the house, the

7.12
Ἡ Πολιτεία

Ὁ μὲν οὖν Ταρκύνιος πέντε καὶ εἴκοσι τυραννήσας ἐνιαυτοὺς οὕτως ἐξέπεσε τῆς ἀρχῆς, οἱ Ῥωμαῖοι δὲ πρὸς τὸν Βροῦτον ἀπέκλιναν καὶ αὐτὸν εἵλοντο ἄρχοντα. ἵνα δὲ μὴ ἡ μοναρχία βασιλεία δοκῇ, καὶ συνάρχοντα αὐτῷ ἐψηφίσαντο τὸν τῆς Λουκρητίας ἐκείνης ἄνδρα τὸν Κολλατῖνον Ταρκύνιον, ὡς ἀπεχθῶς πρὸς τοὺς τυράννους πιστευόμενον ἔχειν διὰ τὴν βίαν τῆς γυναικός. ἐκ δέ γε Ταρκυνίου πρέσβεις εἰς Ῥώμην ἧκον περὶ καθόδου διαλεγόμενοι· ὡς δ᾽ οὐδὲν ἤνυον, ἕτεροι αὖθις ἐπέστησαν, ἀφίστασθαι τῆς βασιλείας καὶ παύειν τὸν πόλεμον λέγοντες τὸν Ταρκύνιον, εἰ τὰ χρήματα δοθεῖεν αὐτῷ καὶ τοῖς φίλοις καὶ τοῖς οἰκείοις, ἀφ᾽ ὧν διαβιώσονται φεύγοντες. ἐπικλωμένων δὲ πολλῶν καὶ αὐτοῦ Κολλατίνου τοῦ τῷ Βρούτῳ συνάρχοντος, εἰς ἀγορὰν ὁ Βροῦτος ἐκ τοῦ βουλευτηρίου ἐξέδραμε, προδότην τὸν Κολλατῖνον ἀποκαλῶν, πολέμου καὶ τυραννίδος ἀφορμὰς χαριζόμενον.

Οἱ πρέσβεις δὲ ἐπὶ τῇ τῶν χρημάτων προφάσει τῇ Ῥώμῃ ἐνδιατρίβοντες ἴσχυσαν διαφθεῖραι τῶν ἐπισήμων τινάς, μεθ᾽ ὧν καὶ δύο τοῦ Βρούτου παῖδας ἔπεισαν ἐν τῇ προδοσίᾳ γενέσθαι. ὡς οὖν συνέπεισαν τὰ μειράκια, ἔδοξε καὶ ὅρκον προβῆναι, καὶ ἐπὶ τούτοις εἰς οἰκίαν συνῆλθον. ἦν δὲ ὁ οἶκος ὑπέρημος καὶ σκοτώδης. ἔλαθεν οὖν ἔνδον ὢν οὐκ ἐκ προνοίας, ἀλλὰ τυχαίως οἰκέτης ὄνομα Οὐινδίκιος, καὶ κατακρυφθεὶς ἐκεῖ θεατής τε τῶν δρωμένων ἦν καὶ τῶν βεβουλευμένων ἐπήκοος· ἅπερ ἦσαν τοὺς ὑπάτους ἀνελεῖν καὶ τὴν πόλιν προδοῦναι· καὶ ταῦτα τῷ Ταρκυνίῳ διὰ τῶν πρέσβεων ἐπεστάλκασιν. ἀπελθόντων δὲ τοῦ οἰκήματος τῶν συνωμοτῶν, ἐξελθὼν ὁ οἰκέτης ἅπαντα

slave left the house and related everything. Those who had planned the treachery were rounded up, and their letters were attended to. They were led to the forum and placed against Vindicius. They recognized their letters. Many stood in dejection and silence, but Brutus called each of his sons by name and asked, "You do not make any defense against the charge?" They held their silence, so Brutus turned to the officers and said, "The rest of the business is yours." They took the youths and beat them to death with their clubs. Although some of the others felt pity for his sons in their suffering, Brutus did not divert his eyes, nor did he display any grief from the beginning until the end, when the executioners removed their heads with an axe. It is not easy either to praise or to blame this action. Either the sublimity of virtue had prompted him to apathy, or the greatness of the suffering drove him to insensibility. Neither of these things is inconsiderable or human – rather, it was either godly or beastly.

After Brutus' sons had died, he ordered that a vote be taken concerning the punishment of the other conspirators. He said, "I have discharged my duty as judge in the case of my sons; I yield the vote concerning the others to the people, who are free." When the vote had been taken, all of the conspirators were killed with axes. Some of these men were the cronies of Collatinus, and he was angered on their account. For that reason, Brutus goaded the people on against him as a minor man, and urged them to murder him with their own hands. They did not do this, but they did compel him to abandon his office. They chose as consul in his place Publius Valerius, who was given the honorary name of Publicola. The name would, converted into Greek, most clearly express that he cared for the people or was on the people's side.

Tarquinius, perceiving the failure of his conspiracy to recover the monarchy, betook himself to the Etruscans. They restored him to considerable power, but the consuls led the Romans against them in

κατεμήνυσε. καὶ οἵ τε τὴν προδοσίαν μελετήσαντες συνελήφθησαν, καὶ τὰ γράμματα ἐκομίσθησαν· καὶ εἰς τὴν ἀγορὰν προαχθέντων αὐτῶν καὶ τὸν Οὐΐνδικα παρεστήσαντο. τά τε γράμματα ἀνεγνώσθησαν· καὶ οἱ μὲν ἄλλοι ἐν κατηφείᾳ ἦσαν καὶ σιωπῇ, ὁ δὲ Βροῦτος ὀνομαστὶ τῶν υἱέων ἑκάτερον προσειπών "οὐκ ἀπολογεῖσθε" ἔφη "πρὸς τὴν κατηγορίαν;" τῶν δὲ σιωπώντων στραφεὶς πρὸς τοὺς ὑπηρέτας "ὑμέτερον" εἶπεν "ἤδη λοιπὸν τὸ ἔργον." οἱ δὲ συλλαβόντες τοὺς νεανίσκους ῥάβδοις κατέξαινον. καὶ τῶν ἄλλων ἐπικλωμένων τοῖς πάσχουσιν ὁ πατὴρ οὔτ' ἀλλαχόσε τὰς ὄψεις ἀπήγαγεν οὔτε μὴν οἴκτου τι ἐνεδείξατο μέχρι πελέκει τὰς κεφαλὰς τῶν παίδων ἀπέκοψαν. τοῦτο δὲ οὔτ' ἐπαινεῖν οὔτε ψέγειν ἐστὶ ῥάδιον· ἢ γὰρ ἀρετῆς ὕψος εἰς ἀπάθειαν ἐξέστησεν αὐτοῦ τὴν ψυχὴν ἢ πάθους μέγεθος εἰς ἀναλγησίαν· οὐδέτερον δὲ μικρὸν οὐδ' ἀνθρώπινον, ἀλλ' ἢ θεῖον ἢ θηριῶδες.

Οὕτω δὲ τούτων θανόντων καὶ περὶ τῶν ἄλλων συνωμοτῶν ψῆφον ἐνεγκεῖν ὁ Βροῦτος ἀπῄτητο. ὁ δέ "τοῖς μὲν υἱέσιν" εἶπεν "αὐτὸς ἀποχρῶν εἰμι δικαστής, περὶ δὲ τῶν ἄλλων τοῖς πολίταις ἐλευθέροις οὖσι τῆς ψήφου παραχωρῶ." ψήφου τοίνυν δοθείσης πάντες ἐπελεκίσθησαν. ἦσαν δὲ τούτων τινὲς τῷ Κολλατίνῳ προσήκοντες· δι' οὓς καὶ ὠργίζετο. ὅθεν ὁ Βροῦτος οὕτω κατ' αὐτοῦ τὸν δῆμον παρώξυνεν ὡς μικροῦ καὶ αὐτοχειρίᾳ αὐτὸν ἀνελεῖν. ἀλλὰ τοῦτο μὲν οὐκ ἐποίησαν, τὴν δ' ἀρχὴν ἠνάγκασαν αὐτὸν ἀπειπεῖν. εἵλοντο δὲ ἀντ' ἐκείνου συνάρχοντα Πόπλιον Οὐαλέριον, ὃς Ποπλικόλας προσωνομάσθη· δηλοῖ δ' ἡ κλῆσις ἐξελληνιζομένη δημοκηδὴ ἢ δημοτικώτατον.

Ταρκύνιος δὲ ἀπογνοὺς τὴν ἐκ προδοσίας τῆς βασιλείας ἀνάληψιν, προσῄει τοῖς Τυρσηνοῖς. οἱ δὲ δυνάμει βαρείᾳ κατῆγον αὐτόν. ἀντεξῆγον δὲ καὶ τοὺς Ῥωμαίους οἱ ὕπατοι. ἀρχομένης δὲ

turn. When the battle began, Arruns, the son of Tarquinius, and Brutus, the Roman consul, fell upon each other in battle. They spared nothing, and died together after fighting with great spirit. After a huge battle and many deaths on both sides, the victory was still unclear. As night came on, it is said that the battleground shook, and a large voice sounded forth saying that in that spot the Etruscans had lost one more man than the Romans. The Romans rose a large, bold war cry upon hearing this sound, and terror seized the Etruscans. In their fear, they withdrew from the battlefield. The Romans seized upon this and plundered the field. They counted the corpses which had fallen in battle, and found that 11,300 Etruscans had died, while the Romans had lost 11,299. Valerius Publicola was then the first Roman consul to hold a triumph.

Tarquinius, following the great battle in which he had lost his son who fought against Brutus, fled to Clusium where he supplicated Lars Porsenna the man with the greatest power among all of the Italic kings; Porsenna then offered to assist him. First, he sent to Rome ordering the Romans to receive Tarquinius, and when they did not obey, he set out with a large force. Valerius Publicola, chosen as consul for a second time and committing himself to the battle, was wounded and drawn from the battle in a litter. As Porsenna was besieging the city, a plague fell upon the Romans. Either from some event, or – as is more likely – from a consideration of the likely outcome, Porsenna broke off the war against the Romans. For a man known as Mucius Cordus, a good man in every way and the noblest warrior, who possessed the cognomen Scaevola (which means either 'one-handed' or 'left-handed') conceived a plan of assassinating Porsenna. He went into the field wearing Etruscan clothing and feigning an Etruscan accent.

τῆς μάχης Ἄρρων ὁ Ταρκυνίου παῖς καὶ Βροῦτος ὁ Ῥωμαίων ὕπατος ἀλλήλοις περιπεσόντες ἐμάχοντο, καὶ ἀφειδήσαντες ὑπὸ θυμοῦ ἑαυτῶν συναπέθανον. μεγάλης δὲ τῆς μάχης γενομένης καὶ πολλῶν ἑκατέρωθεν πεσόντων ἄκριτος ἦν ἡ νίκη. νυκτὸς δ᾽ ἐπελθούσης λέγεται σεισθῆναι τὸ ἄλσος παρ᾽ ᾧ ἐστρατοπεδεύοντο, καὶ φωνὴν ἐκπεσεῖν ἐκεῖθεν μεγάλην φράζουσαν ἑνὶ πλείους τεθνάναι Τυρρηνῶν ἢ Ῥωμαίων. ἅμα δὲ τῇ φωνῇ Ῥωμαῖοι μὲν μέγα καὶ θαρσαλέον ἠλάλαξαν, πτοία δ᾽ ἐνέπεσε Τυρρηνοῖς· καὶ θορυβηθέντες τοῦ στρατοπέδου ἐξέπεσον· εἷλον δ᾽ οἱ Ῥωμαῖοι τοῦτο καὶ διηρπάκασιν. ἀριθμηθέντες δὲ οἱ νεκροὶ τῶν ἐν τῇ μάχῃ θανόντων εὑρέθησαν οἱ μὲν τῶν Τυρρηνῶν ἐπὶ μυρίοις χίλιοι τριακόσιοι, οἱ δὲ Ῥωμαῖοι παρ᾽ ἕνα τοσοῦτοι. ἐθριάμβευσε δὲ Οὐαλέριος Ποπλικόλας πρῶτος ὑπατεύων.

Ὁ δὲ Ταρκύνιος μετὰ τὴν μεγάλην μάχην, ἐν ᾗ καὶ τὸν υἱὸν ἀπέβαλε μαχεσάμενον Βρούτῳ, καταφυγὼν εἰς τὸ Κλούσιον ἱκέτευε Κλάραν Πορσίναν, ἄνδρα μεγίστην ἔχοντα δύναμιν τῶν Ἰταλικῶν βασιλέων· καὶ ὃς αὐτῷ βοηθήσειν ὑπέσχετο. καὶ πρῶτον μὲν ἔπεμψεν εἰς Ῥώμην κελεύων δέχεσθαι τὸν Ταρκύνιον, ὡς δὲ οὐχ ὑπήκουσαν, ἀφίκετο μετὰ βαρείας δυνάμεως. Ποπλικόλας δὲ Οὐαλέριος εἰς ἀρχὴν τὸ δεύτερον αἱρεθεὶς καὶ μάχην συνάψας καὶ τραυματισθεὶς φοράδην τῆς μάχης ἐξεκομίσθη. ἐπικειμένου δὲ τοῦ Πορσίνα τῇ πόλει λιμὸς ἥπτετο τῶν Ῥωμαίων. ἔκ τινος δὲ συμβεβηκότος ἢ μᾶλλον ἐκ προνοίας γενομένου ὁ Πορσίνας τὸν πρὸς Ῥωμαίους κατέλυσε πόλεμον. ἀνὴρ γάρ τις Μούκιος Κόρδος, εἰς πᾶσαν ἀρετὴν ἀγαθός, ἐν δὲ τοῖς πολεμικοῖς ἄριστος, Σκαιόλας τὴν ἐπίκλησιν, ὃ δηλοῖ τὸν μονόχειρα ἢ μὴ ἀρτιόχειρα, τὸν Πορσίναν ἀνελεῖν βουλευσάμενος παρῆλθεν εἰς τὸ ἐκείνου στρατόπεδον, Τυρσηνίδα φορῶν ἐσθῆτα καὶ ὁμοίᾳ κεχρημένος φωνῇ. καὶ

Because he did not know Porsenna's appearance and was afraid to ask, he drew his sword and killed the secretary sitting beside Porsenna and wearing the same type of garment. He was captured and interrogated. A brazier was prepared nearby because Porsenna had been about to make a sacrifice; Scaevola held his hand over the fire, and as his flesh melted away he looked at Porsenna with an unflinching countenance (from this burnt hand his cognomen was derived) until Porsenna, in his astonishment, freed him. Scaevola, however, tried in another way to trick Porsenna and said, "Having conquered your fear, Porsenna, I am your inferior in virtue, and I will therefore disclose freely what I would not have disclosed under compulsion. Three hundred other Romans with the same intention as mine await in the field; I am but the first, having drawn the first lot. I do not feel grieved by fortune, having missed the mark of a good man and one more properly friendly to the Romans than hostile." Thereupon, Porsenna became even more inclined to making a treaty.

Publicola, serving for a third time as consul, continually called Tarquinius to justice, censuring him as the basest man who had rightly fallen from power; Lars Porsenna served as the judge. When Tarquinius responded that he would not accept Porsenna as a judge if he were to be cast off as an ally, Porsenna pronounced his verdict and stopped the war. Even after all of this, the Tarquins tried repeatedly to retake the throne, fighting quite often with the assistance of Rome's neighbors; all of the Tarquins died in these battles, with the exception of the eldest, Tarquinius Superbus. A Greek man would call him, 'ὑπερήφανος' ('the Arrogant'). He later went to Cumae, in Opicia, where he died.

σαφῶς μὲν τὸν Πορσίναν οὐκ εἰδώς, ἐρέσθαι δὲ δεδιώς, τὸν γραμματέα αὐτοῦ συγκαθήμενον αὐτῷ καὶ ὁμοίως ἔχοντα τῆς στολῆς σπασάμενος τὸ ξίφος ἀπέκτεινε, καὶ συλληφθεὶς ἀνεκρίνετο· ἐσχαρίδος δέ τινος τῷ Πορσίνᾳ μέλλοντι θύειν τότε κεκοσμημένης, ὑπερσχὼν τὴν χεῖρα καιομένης τῆς σαρκὸς εἱστήκει πρὸς τὸν Πορσίναν ἀποβλέπων ἀτρέπτῳ προσώπῳ, ὅθεν αὐτῷ τῆς χειρὸς φθαρείσης ἐγένετο ἡ ἐπίκλησις, μέχρι θαυμάσας ἐκεῖνος ἀφῆκεν αὐτόν. ὁ δὲ Σκαιόλας ἕτερον τρόπον ἐσοφίσατο τὸν ἐχθρόν, καὶ εἶπε "τὸν φόβον σου, Πορσίνα, νενικηκὼς ἥττημαί σου τῆς ἀρετῆς, καὶ χάριτι μηνύω ἃ πρὸς ἀνάγκην οὐκ ἂν ἐξηγόρευσα. τριακόσιοι Ῥωμαίων τὴν αὐτὴν ἐμοὶ γνώμην ἔχοντες ἐν τῷ στρατοπέδῳ σου διατρίβουσιν, ὧν ἐγὼ προεπιχειρήσας κλήρῳ λαχὼν οὐκ ἄχθομαι τῇ τύχῃ, διαμαρτὼν ἀνδρὸς ἀγαθοῦ καὶ φίλου μᾶλλον ἢ πολεμίου Ῥωμαίοις εἶναι προσήκοντος." ἐντεῦθεν ὁ Πορσίνας πρὸς τὰς συμβάσεις ἐγένετο προθυμότερος.

Ὁ δὲ Ποπλικόλας τὸ τρίτον ὑπατεύων τότε προυκαλεῖτο συνεχῶς τὸν Ταρκύνιον ἐπὶ δίκῃ, ὡς ἐξελέγξων κάκιστον καὶ ἐκπεπτωκότα τῆς ἀρχῆς ἐνδικώτατα, τοῦ Πορσίνου δικάζοντος. ἀποκριναμένου δὲ Ταρκυνίου μὴ αἱρεῖσθαι Πορσίναν διαιτητήν, εἰ σύμμαχος ὢν μεταβάλλεται, καταγνοὺς ὁ Πορσίνας τὸν πόλεμον κατελύσατο. καὶ μετὰ ταῦτα δὲ πολλάκις μὲν ἐπεχείρησαν οἱ Ταρκύνιοι τὴν βασιλείαν ἀναλαβεῖν, τοῖς ὁμοροῦσι Ῥωμαίοις ἔθνεσι συμμαχούμενοι, πάντες δὲ ἐν ταῖς μάχαις ἐφθάρησαν, πλὴν τοῦ γέροντος, ὃς καὶ Σούπερβος ἐκαλεῖτο· εἴποι ἄν τις Ἕλλην ἀνήρ, ὑπερήφανος. κἀκεῖνος δὲ μετέπειτα εἰς Κύμην τὴν ἐν Ὀπικίᾳ γενόμενος ἐτελεύτησεν.